W9-AQO-763

EYEWITNESS VISUAL DICTIONARIES

THE VISUAL DICTIONARY *of* CHEMISTRY

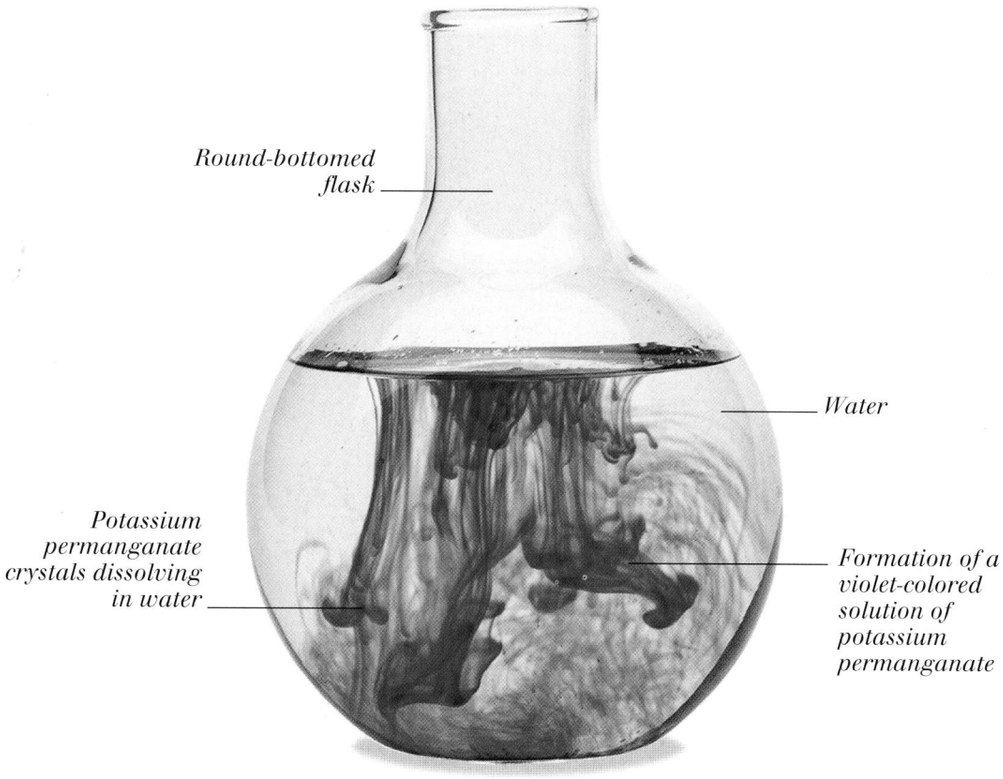

DISSOLVING POTASSIUM PERMANGANATE IN WATER

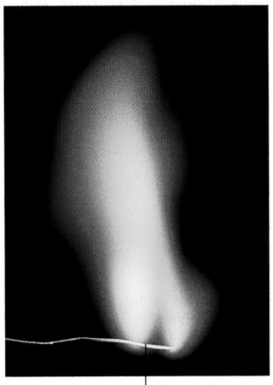

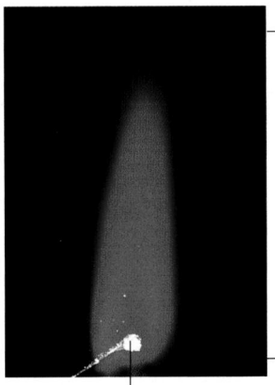

Metal ions color flame

Platinum wire dipped in metal salt solution

Sodium salt

Lead salt

Barium salt

Strontium salt

FLAME TESTS FOR IDENTIFICATION OF METALS

PREPARATION OF NYLON

AQUEOUS SOLUTION

CRYSTALS OF AN IONIC COMPOUND

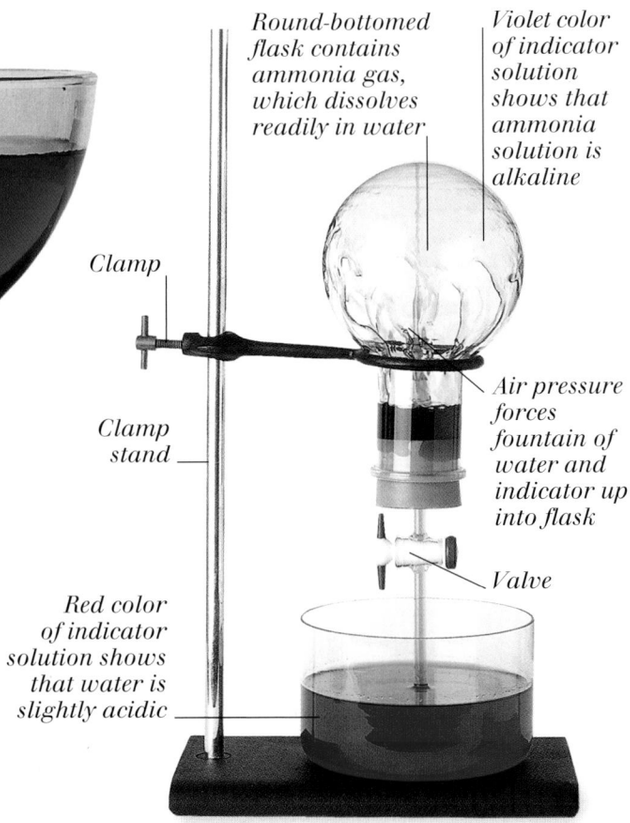

AMMONIA FOUNTAIN EXPERIMENT

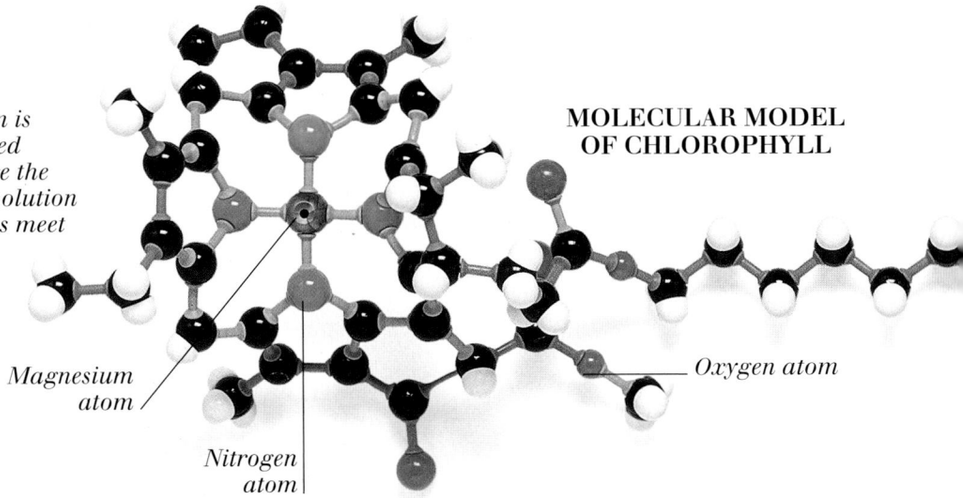

MOLECULAR MODEL OF CHLOROPHYLL

EYEWITNESS VISUAL DICTIONARIES

THE VISUAL DICTIONARY *of* CHEMISTRY

written by
Jack Challoner

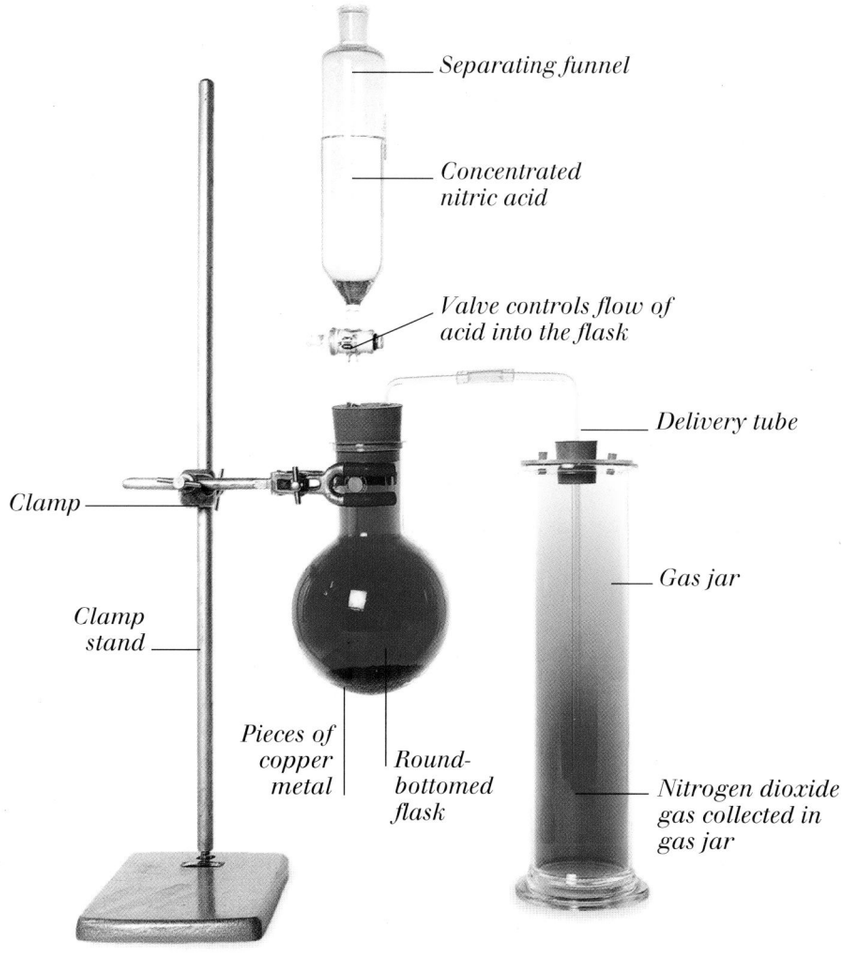

PREPARATION OF NITROGEN DIOXIDE

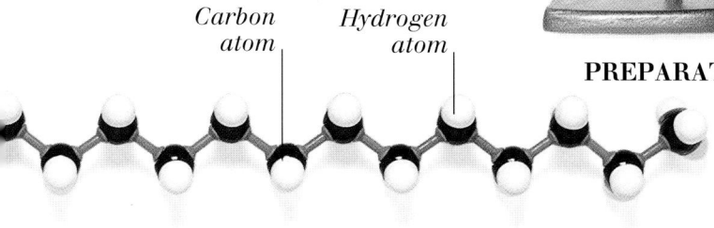

DK

A DK PUBLISHING BOOK

Art Editor Simon Murrell
Project Editor Mukul Patel
Editor Des Reid
Design Assistant Claire Naylor
US Editor Constance M. Robinson
US Consultant Meta Brown

Deputy Art Director Tina Vaughan
Managing Editor Sean Moore
Senior Art Editor Tracy Hambleton-Miles
Senior Editor Louise Candlish

Photography Dean Belcher, Andy Crawford, Tim Ridley
Illustrations Chris Lyon
Production Stephen Stuart

PAPER CHROMATOGRAPHY

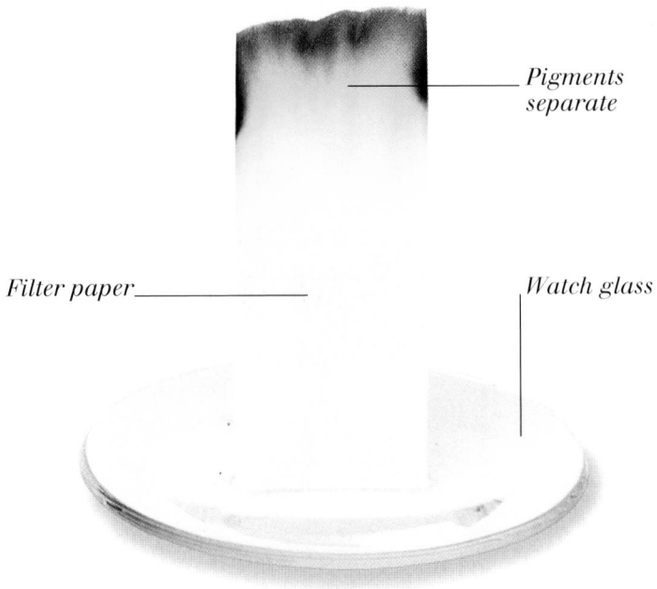

First American Edition 1996
2 4 6 8 10 7 5 3 1
Published in the United States by
DK Publishing, Inc., 95 Madison Avenue, New York, New York 10016
Copyright © 1996 Dorling Kindersley Limited, London
Text Copyright © 1996 Jack Challoner
All rights reserved under International and Pan-American Copyright Conventions. No part of this publication may be reproduced, stored in a retrieval system, or transmitted in any form or by any means, electronic, mechanical, photocopying, recording, or otherwise, without the prior written permission of the copyright owner.
Published in Great Britain by Dorling Kindersley Limited.
Distributed by Houghton Mifflin Company, Boston
Library of Congress Cataloging-in-Publication Data
Challoner, Jack
The visual dictionary of chemistry / written by Jack Challoner.–
1st american ed.
p. cm. – (Eyewitness visual dictionaries)
Includes index.
Summary: Text and illustrations present the fundamentals of chemistry, including such topics as atomic bonds, catalysts, chemical reactions, and various elements.
ISBN 0-7894-0444-3
1. Chemistry–Terminology– Juvenile literature. 2. Chemistry–Pictorial works–Juvenile literature. 3. Picture dictionaries, English–Juvenile literature. [1. Chemistry.] i. Title ii. Series.
QD7.C43 1996 96-52796
540' .3–dc20 CIP
AC

Reproduced by Colourscan, Singapore
Printed and bound by Arnoldo Mondadori, Verona, Italy

WARNING

Do not attempt to carry out any of the experiments shown in this book without the assistance of a trained chemist or chemistry teacher. Some of the experiments produce large amounts of heat or poisonous gases.

SHERWOOD BRANCH LIBRARY

JUN 0 4 1999

Contents

ELEMENTS AND COMPOUNDS 6
MIXTURES 8
ATOMS AND MOLECULES 10
PERIODIC TABLE 12
METALS AND NONMETALS 14
BONDS BETWEEN ATOMS 16
CHEMICAL REACTIONS 18
OXIDATION AND REDUCTION 20
ACIDS AND BASES 22
SALTS 24
CATALYSTS 26
HEAT IN CHEMISTRY 28
WATER IN CHEMISTRY 30
THE ACTIVITY SERIES 32
ELECTROCHEMISTRY 34
THE ALKALI METALS 36
THE ALKALINE EARTH METALS 38
TRANSITION METALS 40
CARBON, SILICON, AND TIN 42
NITROGEN AND PHOSPHORUS 44
OXYGEN AND SULFUR 46
THE HALOGENS 48
ORGANIC CHEMISTRY 1 50
ORGANIC CHEMISTRY 2 52
CHEMICAL ANALYSIS 54
USEFUL DATA 56
GLOSSARY 57
INDEX 60
ACKNOWLEDGMENTS 64

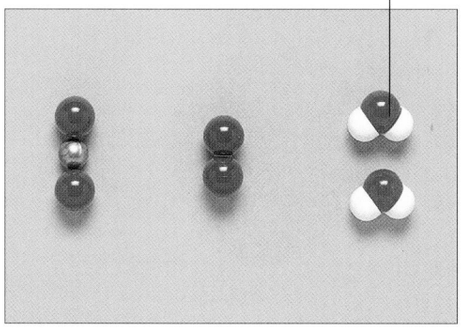

MOLECULAR MODEL OF REACTION

IONIC COMPOUND

COBALT(II) CHLORIDE

DISPLACEMENT REACTION

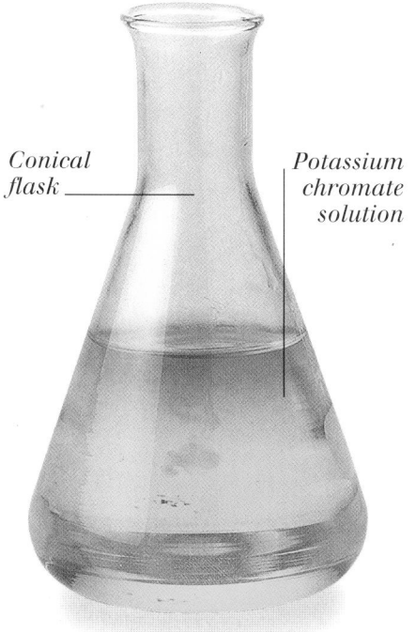

REVERSIBLE REACTION

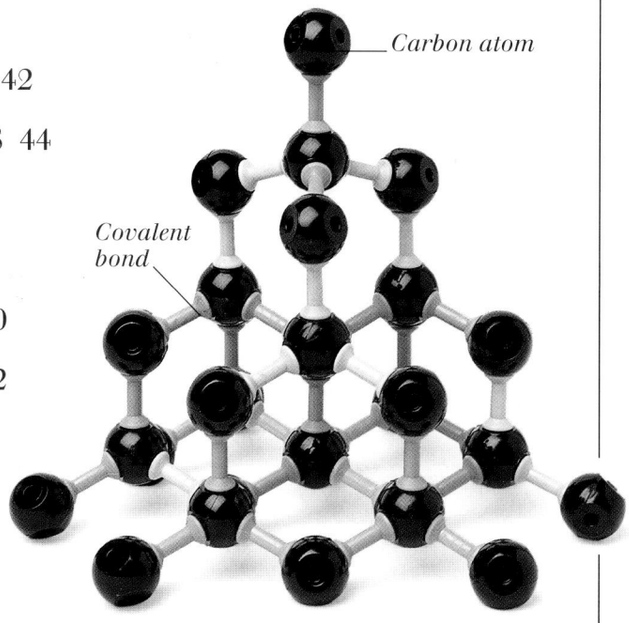

MOLECULAR STRUCTURE OF DIAMOND

B.2 # 1895 06/99 Sherwood

Elements and compounds

CHEMISTRY IS THE STUDY OF MATTER. All ordinary matter consists of tiny units called **atoms** (see pp. 10–11). An **element** is a substance that contains atoms of one type only. However, pure elements are rarely found in nature – they are nearly always combined with other elements. A **compound** is a substance in which the atoms of two or more elements are combined in definite proportions. The atoms in a compound are often bound together in units called **molecules**. For example, each molecule of the compound ammonia, NH_3, consists of one atom of nitrogen, N, bound to three of hydrogen, H. Atoms interact with each other during **chemical reactions**, making or breaking bonds to form new substances. The **products** of a reaction often have very different properties than the original **reactants**. For example, iron, a magnetic element, reacts with the yellow element sulfur to produce iron(II) sulfide, which is neither magnetic nor yellow. Similarly, the compound mercury(II) oxide is an orange powder – very different from its constituent elements.

A SELECTION OF ELEMENTS AND COMPOUNDS
These pure samples of elements and compounds show the diversity of substances found in nature.

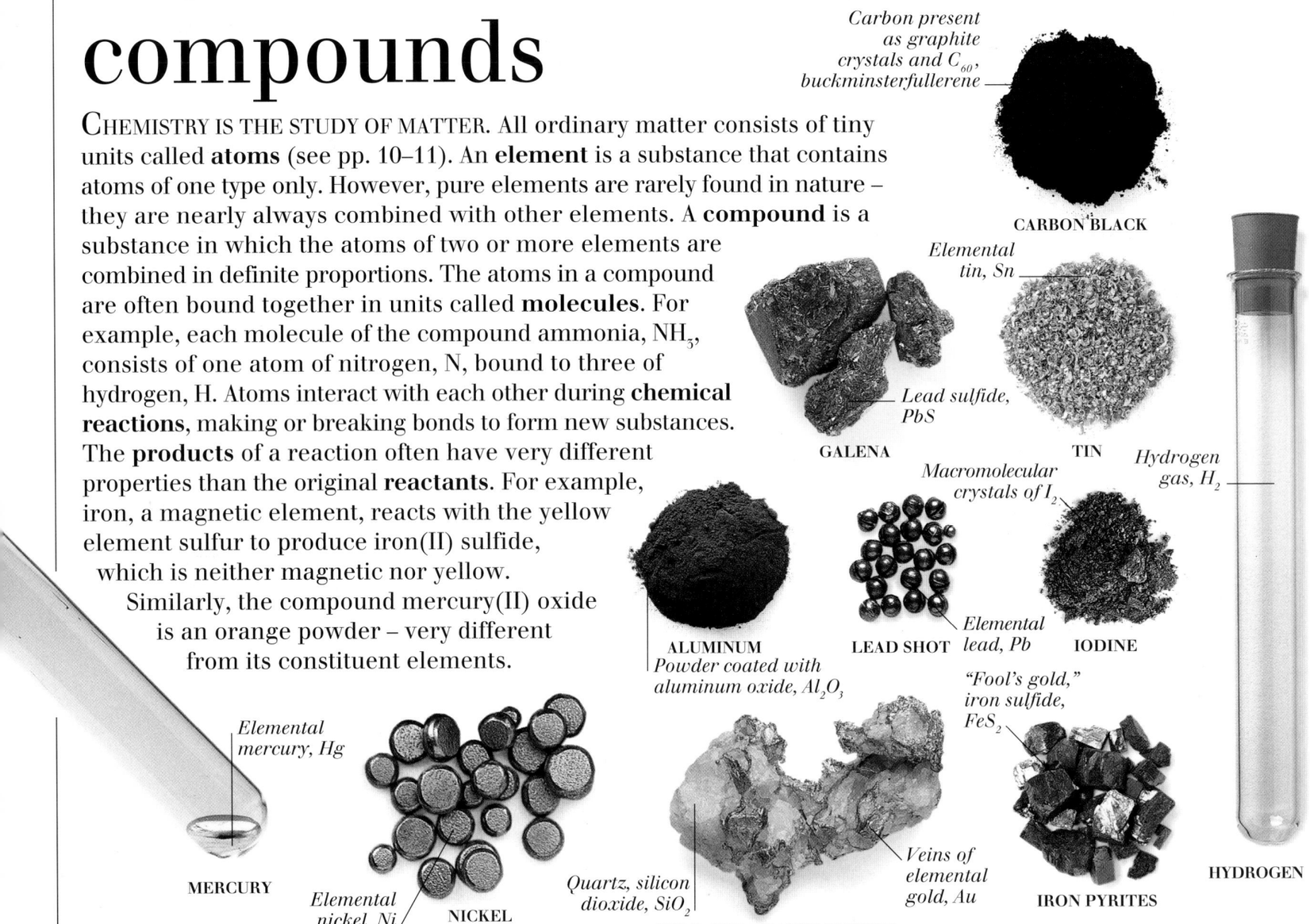

MOLECULAR MODELS
Many compounds exist as individual molecules. Models of molecules can help us to understand and predict chemical reactions. Space-filling models show how the atoms that make up a molecule overlap. Ball and stick models show the bonds and bond angles between the atoms.

MOLECULES

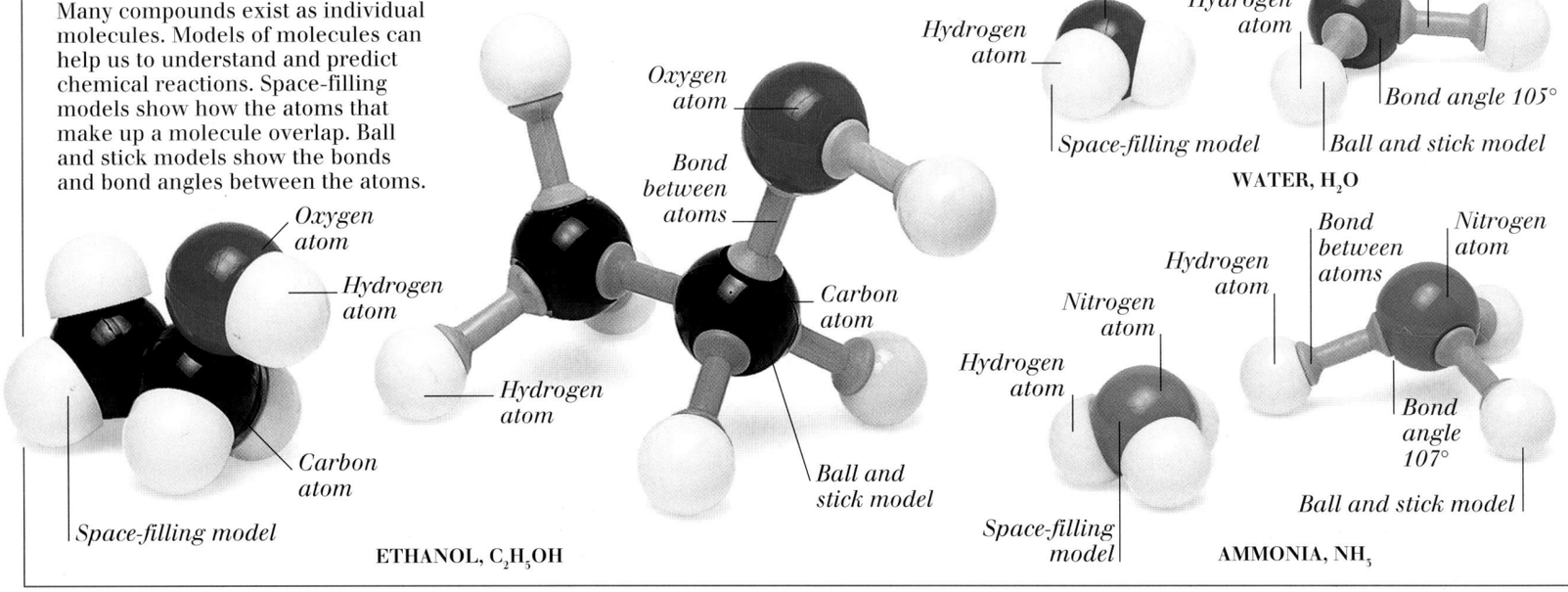

PREPARATION OF IRON(II) SULFIDE

CHEMICAL REACTION
Heating the elements iron and sulfur together causes a chemical reaction to occur. The iron and sulfur combine in the ratio 1:1 to form the compound iron(II) sulfide. With equal numbers of iron and sulfur atoms, the elements would combine with no residue.

Test tube

Sulfur and iron atoms in roughly equal numbers

Sulfur

Iron

CORRECT PROPORTIONS

Not all of the sulfur can react

Sulfur

Not all of the iron can react

Iron

EXCESS IRON

EXCESS SULFUR

Clamp stand

Clamp

Test tube

Unreacted sulfur

Iron(II) sulfide

RESULT WITH EXCESS SULFUR

IRON(II) SULFIDE
Iron and sulfur chemically combine to form iron(II) sulfide, FeS, which is a gray, nonmagnetic solid at room temperature.

MIXING IRON AND SULFUR

Magnetic iron and yellow sulfur retain their properties, and can be easily separated, in a **mixture** (see pp. 8–9).

Iron and sulfur mixed but not chemically combined

MIXTURE OF IRON AND SULFUR

Magnet attracts iron filings

Yellow sulfur left behind

Watch glass

SEPARATING THE MIXTURE

Iron(II) sulfide

No residue

RESULT USING CORRECT PROPORTIONS

Unreacted iron

Iron(II) sulfide

RESULT WITH EXCESS IRON

MERCURY(II) OXIDE

DECOMPOSITION
When heated, the compound mercury(II) oxide **decomposes** to produce its constituent elements, mercury and oxygen. The heat provides the **energy** needed to break the bonds between the atoms of the two elements. The oxygen is a gas at room temperature, and escapes into the air.

Clamp stand

Oxygen escapes from tube

Clamp

Flame provides heat

Clamp stand base

Bunsen burner

Test tube

Beads of mercury

This form of mercury(II) oxide is an orange powder

Oxygen atom

Mercury atom

Mercury(II) oxide → mercury metal + oxygen gas

$2HgO \rightarrow 2Hg + O_2$

Oxygen molecule

MOLECULAR MODEL OF REACTION

CLOSE-UP VIEW
A closer view of the reaction shows tiny beads of the mercury metal produced. The models above present a molecular view of the reaction, while the equation summarizes the reaction symbolically.

Mixtures

A MIXTURE CONTAINS TWO or more pure substances (**elements** or **compounds**), which may be solids, liquids, or gases. For example, air is a **mixture** of gases, cement is a mixture of solids, and seawater is a mixture of solids, liquids, and gases. A **solution** is a common type of mixture, consisting of a **solute** (often a solid) mixed evenly with a **solvent** (usually liquid). When the solvent is water, the solute particles are usually **ions**. Other types of mixtures include **colloids**, like milk, in which the dispersed particles are slightly larger than ions, and **suspensions**, in which they are larger still. Because the substances making up a mixture are not chemically combined (see pp. 16–17), they can be separated easily. **Chromatography** is used to separate mixtures for analysis, for example in Breathalyzers. A technique called **filtration** is used to separate suspensions such as muddy water. Solutions may be separated by **distillation**, in which the solvent is boiled off and collected, and the solute is left behind. If both the solute and the solvent are liquids, then a technique called fractional distillation is used (see pp. 50–51).

AIR AS A MIXTURE

The colored balls in this column represent the proportions of gases in dry air. Usually, air also contains water vapor and dust particles.

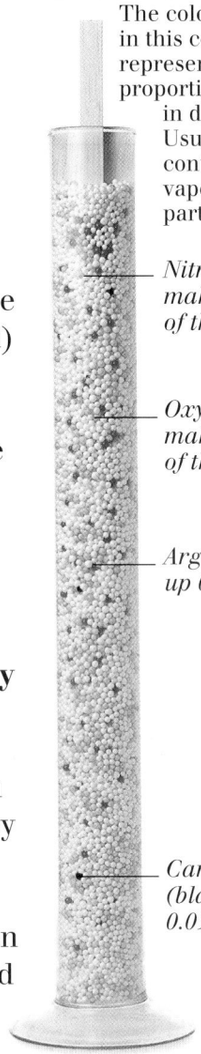

SOLUTIONS

Nickel(II) nitrate is a solid at room temperature. It dissolves well in water to give a green-colored **aqueous solution**.

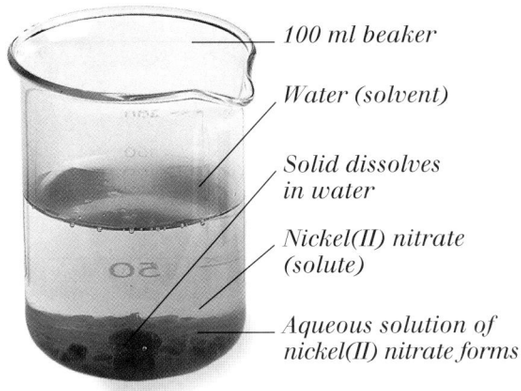

SOLUTION OF NICKEL(II) NITRATE IN WATER

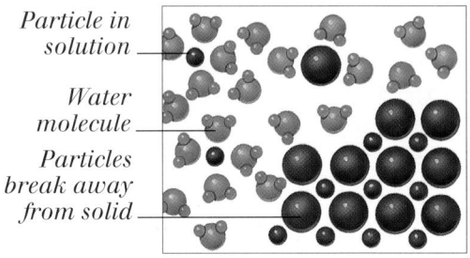

MICROSCOPIC VIEW

When a solid dissolves in a liquid solvent such as water, the particles of the solid break away and mix evenly and thoroughly with particles of the liquid.

PAPER CHROMATOGRAPHY

Ink from a felt-tip pen is dissolved in alcohol in a glass dish. The alcohol soaks into the absorbent filter paper, carrying the ink with it. Colored ink is a mixture of several pigments, which bind to the paper to different extents. Those pigments that bind loosely move more quickly up the paper than the others, so the ink separates into its constituent pigments.

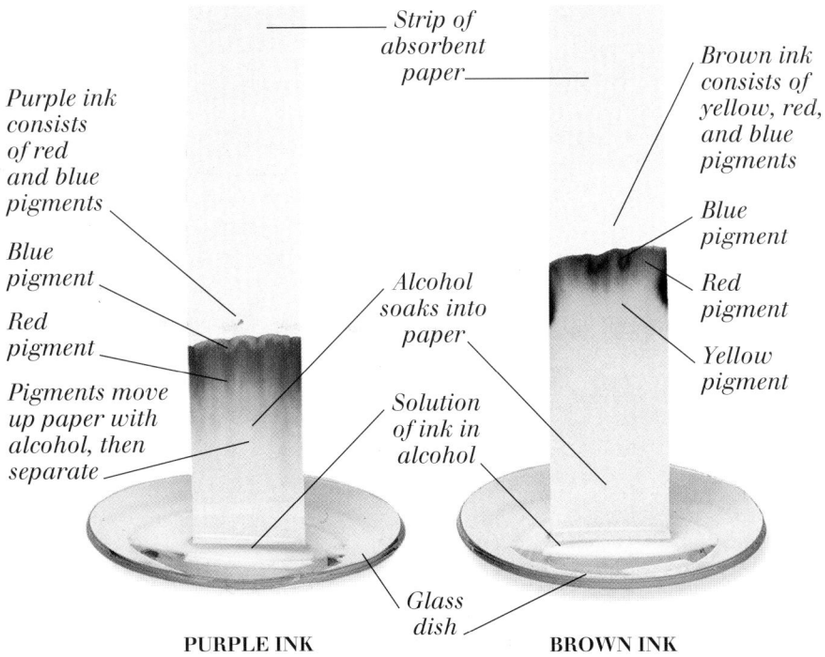

GAS CHROMATOGRAPHY

The sample for analysis is vaporized and carried through a granulated solid by a moving stream of an inert gas such as helium. Different parts of the sample travel at different rates through the solid, and can be identified by a sensitive detector.

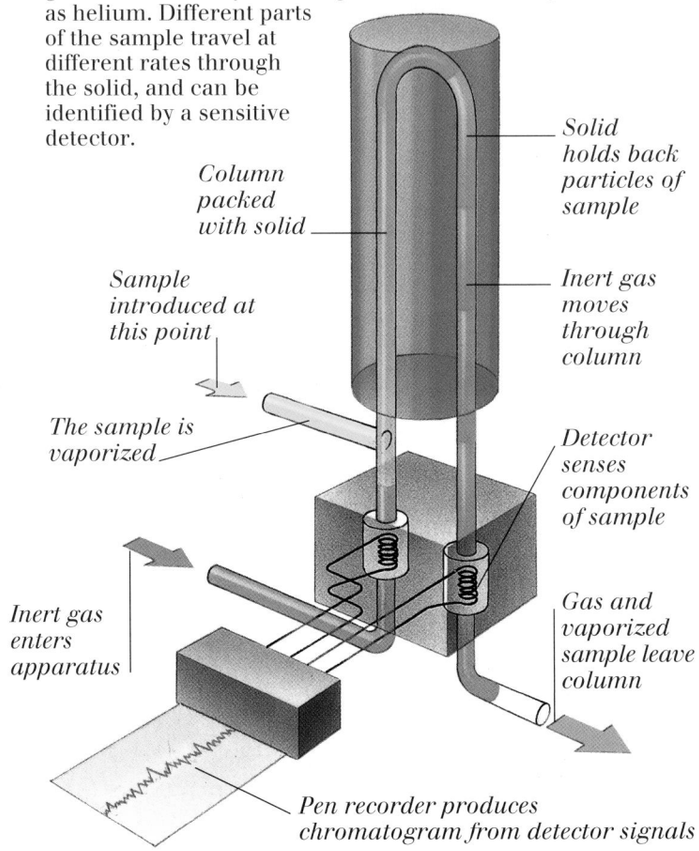

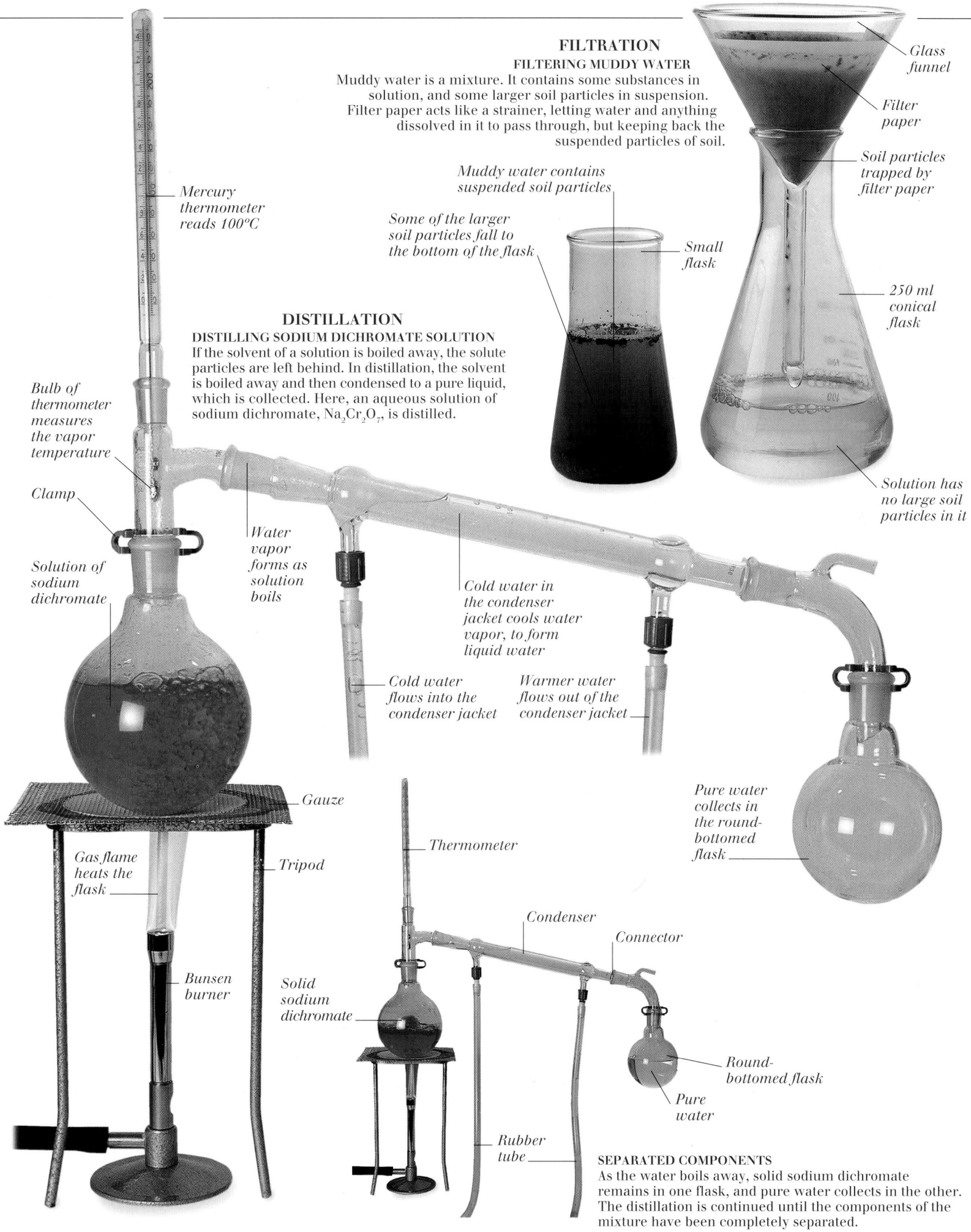

FILTRATION

FILTERING MUDDY WATER

Muddy water is a mixture. It contains some substances in solution, and some larger soil particles in suspension. Filter paper acts like a strainer, letting water and anything dissolved in it to pass through, but keeping back the suspended particles of soil.

DISTILLATION

DISTILLING SODIUM DICHROMATE SOLUTION

If the solvent of a solution is boiled away, the solute particles are left behind. In distillation, the solvent is boiled away and then condensed to a pure liquid, which is collected. Here, an aqueous solution of sodium dichromate, $Na_2Cr_2O_7$, is distilled.

SEPARATED COMPONENTS

As the water boils away, solid sodium dichromate remains in one flask, and pure water collects in the other. The distillation is continued until the components of the mixture have been completely separated.

Atoms and molecules

EVERY ATOM CONTAINS AN equal number of **electrically charged protons** and **electrons**, and a number of uncharged **neutrons**. Neutrons and the positively charged protons are found in the central **nucleus**. The nucleus is surrounded by negatively charged electrons, which take part in chemical bonding (see pp. 16–17). Each **element** has a unique **atomic number** – the number of protons in its **atoms** – though the number of neutrons varies between different **isotopes** of the element. An atom's mass may be given simply as the total number of neutrons and protons, since these particles have nearly equal masses, far greater than that of an electron. The **relative atomic mass (RAM)** is a more precise measure, based on the accurately determined atomic mass of a carbon isotope. The sum of the RAMs of the elements making up a **compound** is called the **relative molecular mass (RMM)**. One **mole** of a substance has the same mass in grams as its RAM or RMM. The mole is a useful unit, because it specifies a fixed number of atoms, **ions**, or **molecules**.

ATOM OF BORON
Every boron atom has five electrons in two **electron shells** around the nucleus. In each shell, electrons are most likely to be found in regions known as **orbitals**.

One electron in 2p-orbital of second electron shell

Two electrons in 2s-orbital of second electron shell

Proton

Nucleus

Neutron

Two electrons in 1s-orbital of first electron shell

Each orbital contains up to two electrons

Electrical forces between protons and electrons hold atom together

ATOMIC ORBITALS

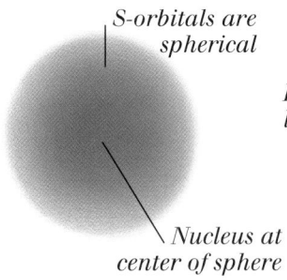

S-ORBITAL

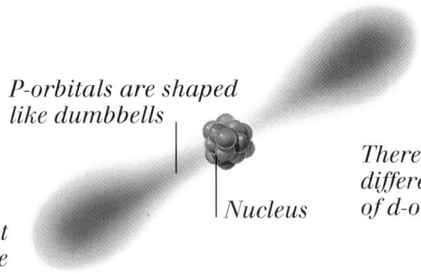

P-ORBITAL

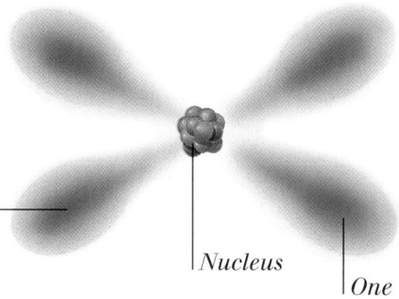

D-ORBITAL

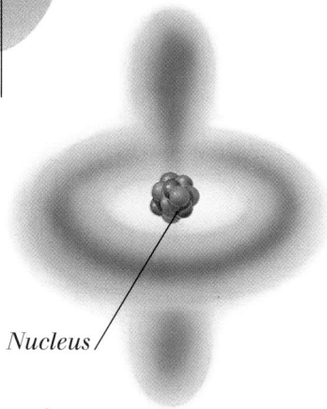

D-ORBITAL

RELATIVE ATOMIC MASS (RAM)

NUCLEUS OF BORON-10

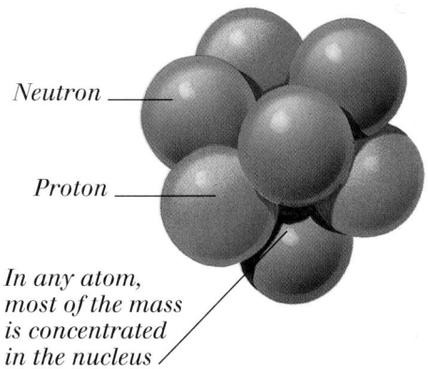

ISOTOPES
An element's atoms are found in various chemically identical forms called isotopes, which differ only in the number of neutrons in the nucleus. Different natural samples of an element have the same proportions of the different isotopes. An element's RAM takes into account the natural abundances of different isotopes. The RAM for boron is just less than 11 (actually, 10.8), since most of the atoms in nature are of boron-11.

NUCLEUS OF BORON-11

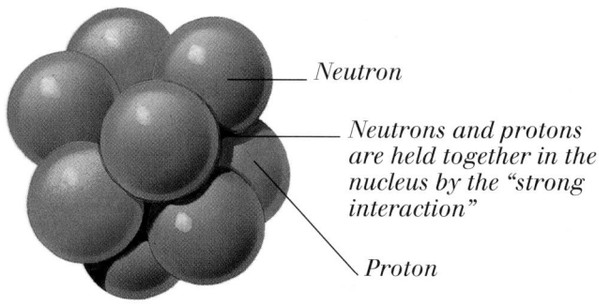

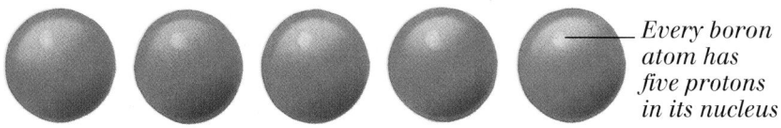

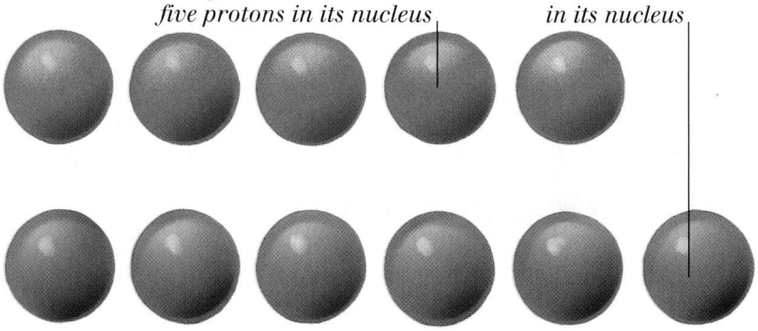

GAS MOLAR VOLUME

One mole of any gas at STP would fill up more than 22 of these bottles

1 LITER BOTTLE

BOX CONTAINING ONE MOLE OF GAS

GAS VOLUME AT STP
One mole of any gas at standard temperature and pressure (**STP**) always occupies 22.4 liters of space. Although the number of particles (atoms or molecules) making up one mole of a gas is extremely large, each particle is very tiny. This means that the volume of a gas depends upon only the number of particles present, and not on the size of each particle. The box and the bottle (left) give an idea of the molar volume of any gas at STP.

MOLAR MASSES

ONE MOLE OF COPPER
Copper has an RAM of 64.4, so the molar mass of copper is 64.4 grams. The number of atoms present is 6.02×10^{23}.

64.4 grams of copper (one mole)

Copper is a metallic element

126.9 grams of iodine (one mole)

ONE MOLE OF IODINE
The element iodine has an RAM of 126.9. The molar mass of iodine is 126.9 grams. The number of atoms, ions, or molecules in one mole of any substance is 6.02×10^{23} – a number known as Avogadro's constant.

Iodine is a violet solid at room temperature

0.1 MOLE OF COBALT CHLORIDE
The RMM of hydrated cobalt chloride, $CoCl_2.6H_2O$, is 226.9, obtained by adding the RAMs of each of the atoms making up the compound. Here, a chemical balance is used to measure accurately 0.1 mole of the substance, which has a mass of 22.69 grams.

The balance has been tared, or set to zero, with the empty beaker on the pan, so that the mass of the sample is displayed

50 ml beaker

Pan

Cobalt chloride is a red solid at room temperature

Accurate chemical balance

Digital readout shows that the mass of the sample is 22.69 grams

PREPARING A 0.1 M SOLUTION OF COBALT CHLORIDE

Plastic stopper

0.1 MOLAR SOLUTION OF COBALT CHLORIDE
Enough water is mixed thoroughly with 0.1 mole of cobalt chloride (below left) to make exactly one liter of **solution**. The cobalt chloride dissolves to form a 0.1 molar (0.1M) solution. This is the **concentration** of the solution, sometimes known as its molarity.

Volumetric flask

Neck of flask is narrow, so that it may be accurately filled

Etched mark on flask indicates 1 liter capacity

Solution of cobalt chloride

The periodic table

THE CHEMICAL ELEMENTS CAN BE arranged according to their **atomic number** (the number of **protons** in the **nuclei** of their **atoms**) and the way in which their **electrons** are organized. The result is the periodic table. **Elements** at the beginning of each horizontal row, or period, have one electron in the outer **electron shell** of their atoms (see pp. 10–11). All of the elements in each vertical column, or group, of the table have similar chemical properties because they all have the same number of outer electrons. The elements of the last group of the table, group 18, have full outer electron shells, and are inert, or unreactive. These elements are called the **noble gases**. Moving down the table, the length of the periods increases in steps, because as the atoms become larger, more types of electron **orbitals** become available. Periods six and seven are 32 elements long, but for simplicity a series of elements from each of these periods is placed separately under the main table.

Group 1	Group 2	Group 3	Group 4	Group 5	Group 6	Group 7	Group 8	Group 9
1 H Hydrogen 1.0								
3 Li Lithium 6.9	4 Be Beryllium 9.0							
11 Na Sodium 23.0	12 Mg Magnesium 24.3							
19 K Potassium 39.1	20 Ca Calcium 40.1	21 Sc Scandium 45.0	22 Ti Titanium 47.9	23 V Vanadium 50.9	24 Cr Chromium 52.0	25 Mn Manganese 54.9	26 Fe Iron 55.9	27 Co Cobalt 58.9
37 Rb Rubidium 85.5	38 Sr Strontium 87.6	39 Y Yttrium 88.9	40 Zr Zirconium 91.2	41 Nb Niobium 92.9	42 Mo Molybdenum 95.9	43 Tc Technetium (99)	44 Ru Ruthenium 101.0	45 Rh Rhodium 102.9
55 Cs Cesium 132.9	56 Ba Barium 137.3	57-71	72 Hf Hafnium 178.5	73 Ta Tantalum 180.9	74 W Tungsten 183.9	75 Re Rhenium 186.2	76 Os Osmium 190.2	77 Ir Iridium 192.2
87 Fr Francium 223.0	88 Ra Radium 226.0	89-103	104 Unq Unnilquadium (261)	105 Unp Unnilpentium (262)	106 Unh Unnilhexium (263)	107 Uns Unnilseptium (262)	108 Uno Unniloctium (265)	109 Une Unnilennium (266)

s-block *d-block*

Relative atomic mass is estimated, as element exists fleetingly

Disputes over the discovery and naming of elements 104–109 have led to temporary systematic Latin names

57 La Lanthanum 138.9	58 Ce Cerium 140.1	59 Pr Praseodymium 140.9	60 Nd Neodymium 144.2	61 Pm Promethium (145)	62 Sm Samarium 150.4
89 Ac Actinium 227.0	90 Th Thorium 232.0	91 Pa Protactinium 231.0	92 U Uranium 238.0	93 Np Neptunium (237)	94 Pu Plutonium (242)

f-block

KEY TO TYPES OF ELEMENT

- ALKALI METALS
- ALKALINE EARTH METALS
- TRANSITION METALS
- LANTHANIDES (RARE EARTHS)
- ACTINIDES
- POOR METALS
- SEMIMETALS
- NONMETALS
- NOBLE GASES

ARTIFICIAL ELEMENTS

Uranium, atomic number 92, is the heaviest element found on Earth. Heavier elements are inherently unstable, because the nuclei of their atoms are too large to hold together. The transuranic elements, atomic numbers 93 to 109, are only produced artificially in the laboratory.

NOBLE GASES

Group 18, on the right of the table, contains elements whose atoms have filled outer electron shells. This means that they are inert elements, reacting with other substances only under extreme conditions, and so forming few **compounds**.

Atomic number
Chemical symbol
Name of element
Relative atomic mass

Group 10	Group 11	Group 12	Group 13	Group 14	Group 15	Group 16	Group 17	Group 18
								2 He Helium 4.0
			5 B Boron 10.8	6 C Carbon 12.0	7 N Nitrogen 14.0	8 O Oxygen 16.0	9 F Fluorine 19.0	10 Ne Neon 20.2
			13 Al Aluminum 27.0	14 Si Silicon 28.1	15 P Phosphorus 31.0	16 S Sulfur 32.1	17 Cl Chlorine 35.5	18 Ar Argon 40.0
28 Ni Nickel 58.7	29 Cu Copper 63.5	30 Zn Zinc 65.4	31 Ga Gallium 69.7	32 Ge Germanium 72.6	33 As Arsenic 74.9	34 Se Selenium 79.0	35 Br Bromine 79.9	36 Kr Krypton 83.8
46 Pd Palladium 106.4	47 Ag Silver 107.9	48 Cd Cadmium 112.4	49 In Indium 114.8	50 Sn Tin 118.7	51 Sb Antimony 121.8	52 Te Tellurium 127.6	53 I Iodine 126.9	54 Xe Xenon 131.3
78 Pt Platinum 195.1	79 Au Gold 197.0	80 Hg Mercury 200.6	81 Tl Thallium 204.4	82 Pb Lead 207.2	83 Bi Bismuth 209.0	84 Po Polonium 210.0	85 At Astatine (211)	86 Rn Radon 222.0

d-block *p-block*

Different blocks of the periodic table contain elements whose atoms have different orbitals in their outer electron shells

Lanthanides and actinides placed separately from rest of periods six and seven

Moving to the adjacent element along a period, atomic number increases by one

63 Eu Europium 152.0	64 Gd Gadolinium 157.3	65 Tb Terbium 158.9	66 Dy Dysprosium 162.5	67 Ho Holmium 164.9	68 Er Erbium 167.3	69 Tm Thulium 168.9	70 Yb Ytterbium 173.0	71 Lu Lutetium 175.0
95 Am Americium (243)	96 Cm Curium (247)	97 Bk Berkelium (247)	98 Cf Californium (251)	99 Es Einsteinium (254)	100 Fm Fermium (253)	101 Md Mendelevium (256)	102 No Nobelium (254)	103 Lr Lawrencium (257)

f-block

Metals and nonmetals

MOST OF THE ELEMENTS ARE METALS. Metals are usually lustrous (shiny), and, apart from copper and gold, are silver or gray in color. They are all good conductors of heat and electricity, and are ductile (capable of being drawn into wire) and malleable (capable of being hammered into sheets) to different extents. Found at the left-hand side of the periodic table (see pp. 12–13), metals have few outer **electrons**, which they easily lose to form **cations**. Their **compounds** generally exhibit **ionic bonding** (see pp. 16–17). Most nonmetals are gases at room temperature, and generally form **anions**. Many simple ionic compounds are formed by metal **atoms** losing electrons to nonmetals, and the resulting ions bonding to form **macromolecules**. Sodium and chlorine react in this way to form sodium chloride. In nature, most metals are found not as **elements**, but in compounds known as **ores**. Most metals easily combine with oxygen to form metal oxides, and many ores consist of metal oxides. The simple removal of oxygen is enough to extract a metal from such an ore. The more **reactive** a metal is, the more **energy** is needed for its extraction. Iron can be extracted relatively easily from iron oxide, while more reactive sodium must be extracted by a powerful electric current.

METALLIC ELEMENTS

TIN

ALUMINUM POWDER

COPPER TURNINGS

MAGNESIUM RIBBON

Magnesium, a typical metal, is ductile

CATIONS AND ANIONS

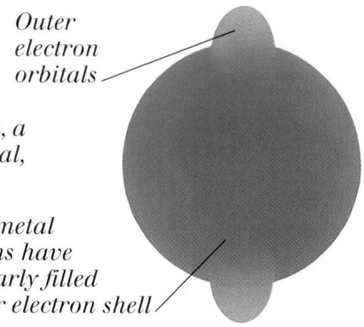

NONMETAL ATOM

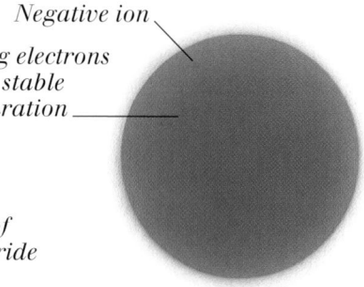

NONMETAL ANION

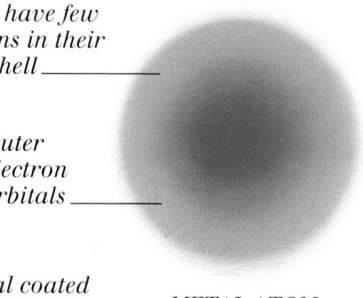

METAL ATOM

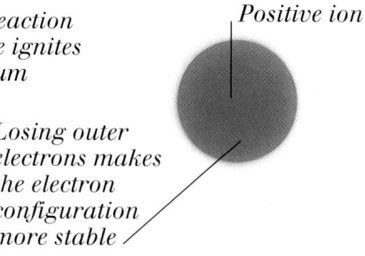

METAL CATION

FORMATION OF SODIUM CHLORIDE FROM ITS ELEMENTS

When metallic sodium, Na, is gently heated and placed in the nonmetallic gas chlorine, Cl_2, a violent **exothermic reaction** occurs. The **product** of the reaction is sodium chloride, NaCl – the familiar white **crystals** of common salt.

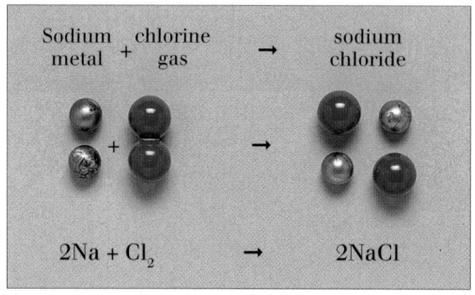

MOLECULAR VIEW
Each chlorine **molecule** has two chlorine atoms. Two sodium atoms react with each chlorine molecule, to form sodium chloride (see p. 17). Electrons are transferred from the sodium atoms to the chlorine atoms.

Gas jar

Chlorine gas

CHLORINE GAS
Chlorine is a greenish yellow poisonous gas at room temperature. It is in group 17 of the periodic table.

SODIUM METAL
Like most metals, sodium is silver gray. It is a soft metal, found in group 1 of the periodic table.

Sodium is easily cut, exposing its luster

Tiny pieces of sodium chloride form smoke in the jar

Sodium metal coated with a layer of sodium chloride

Heat of the reaction with chlorine ignites piece of sodium

Sodium chloride

SODIUM CHLORIDE
Sodium chloride is a white solid at room temperature. It consists of macromolecules.

EXTRACTION OF METALS

IRON FROM IRON OXIDE
Carbon can be used to extract iron from the compound iron oxide, which is found in many iron ores. The reaction needs a relatively low input of heat energy in order to proceed.

REACTANTS

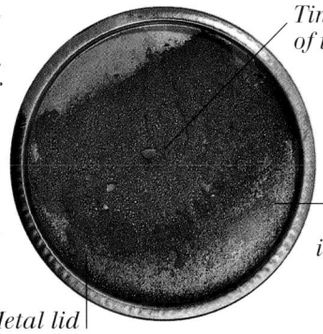

PRODUCTS

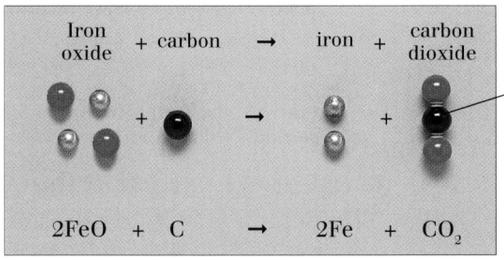

MOLECULAR VIEW
Iron oxide is **decomposed** by heat. The oxygen atoms produced bond to carbon atoms, forming carbon dioxide gas. This is a **redox reaction**.

THE DOWNS PROCESS
The industrial-scale extraction of sodium metal is normally achieved by the **electrolysis** of molten sodium chloride. In the Downs Process, a small amount of calcium chloride is added to the sodium chloride to lower its melting point.

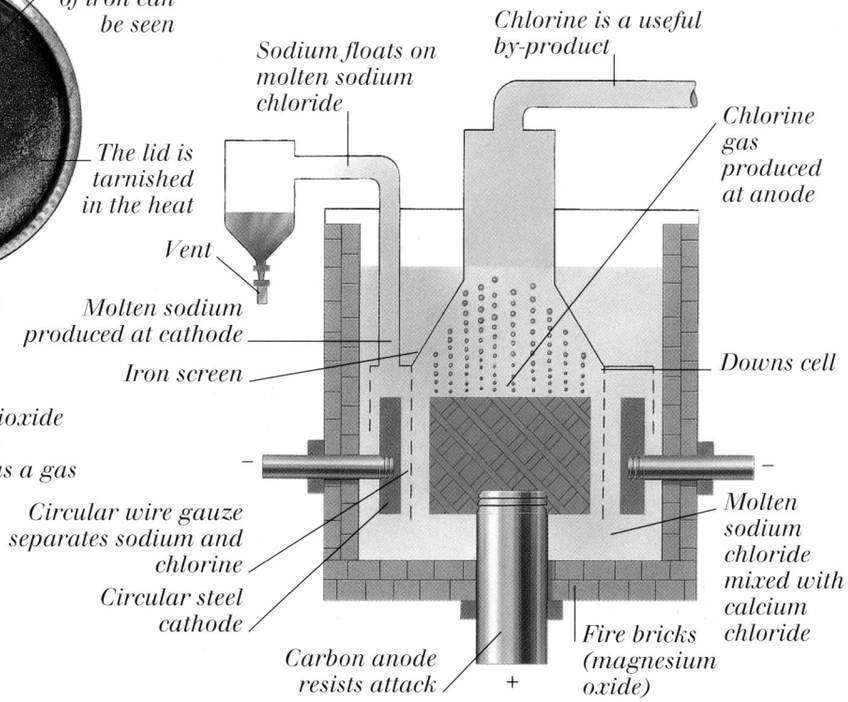

METALS AND OXYGEN

BURNING MAGNESIUM
In the reverse process of extraction from metal oxides, most pure metals readily combine with oxygen. Here, magnesium ribbon **burns** with a bright white flame as it reacts with oxygen from the air. Magnesium is used in fireworks (see pp. 38–39), and was once common in photographic flash bulbs.

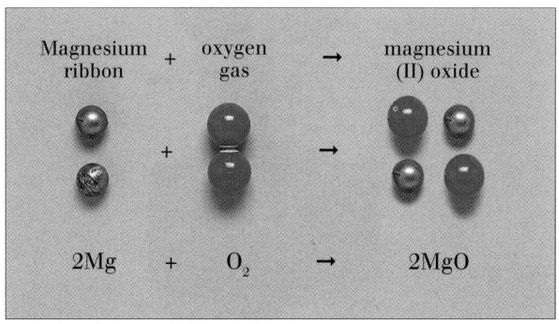

MOLECULAR VIEW
Magnesium ribbon consists of millions of magnesium atoms, Mg, only. Oxygen in the air exists as **diatomic** molecules. During the reaction, bonds form between the magnesium atoms and oxygen atoms.

MAGNESIUM(II) OXIDE ASH
After burning, an ash of magnesium(II) oxide, MgO, is left. This is a white compound of magnesium (a metal) and oxygen (a nonmetal).

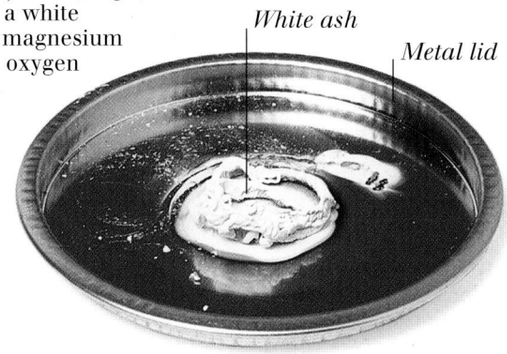

Bonds between atoms

ATOMS CAN JOIN – OR BOND – in many ways. Instruments called **atomic force microscopes** produce images of actual **atoms**, revealing these bonds. The two most important types of bonding are **ionic bonding** and **covalent bonding**. **Compounds** are referred to as ionic or covalent depending on the type of bonding that they exhibit. In ionic bonding, a transfer of **electrons** from one atom to another creates two **ions** with opposing **electric charge**. The transfer is generally from a metal to a nonmetal (see pp. 14–15). Electrostatic attraction between the ions of opposite charge holds them together. Ionic compounds form **macromolecules** – giant structures consisting of millions of ions. A familiar example of an ionic compound is sodium chloride (common salt). Each grain of common salt is a macromolecule. Atoms that are bound covalently share electrons in their outer **electron shells**. These shared electrons are found within regions called **molecular orbitals**. Another important type of bonding, **hydrogen bonding**, occurs between **molecules** of many hydrogen-containing compounds, and is the cause of some of the unusual properties of water.

ATOMIC FORCE MICROSCOPE IMAGE

This image shows atoms of gold on a graphite surface. The colors are added to the image for clarity. The graphite atoms are joined by covalent bonds.

COVALENT AND IONIC COMPOUNDS

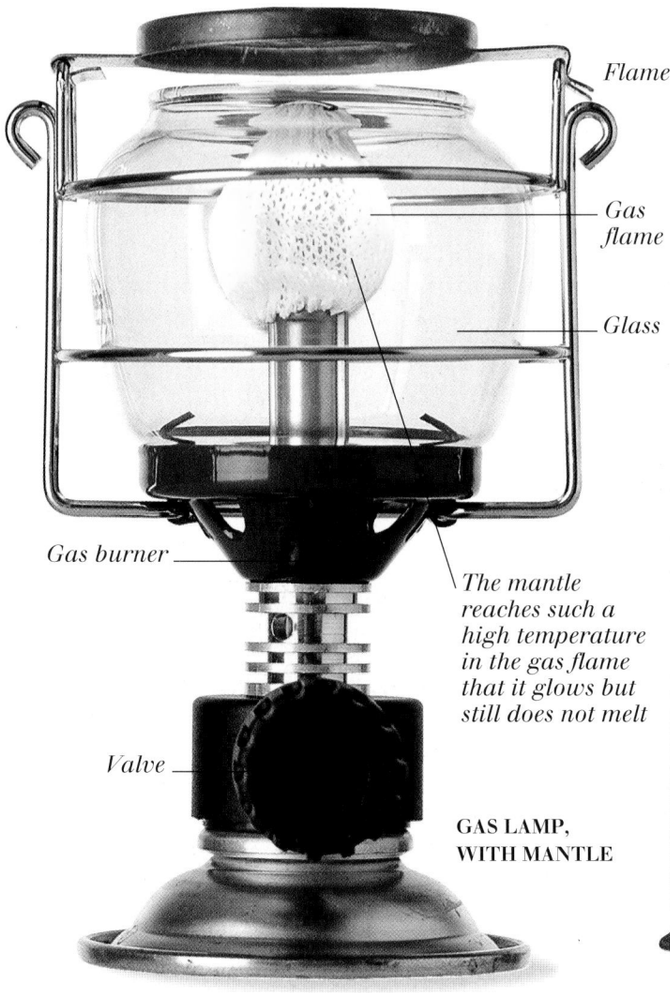

GAS LAMP, WITH MANTLE

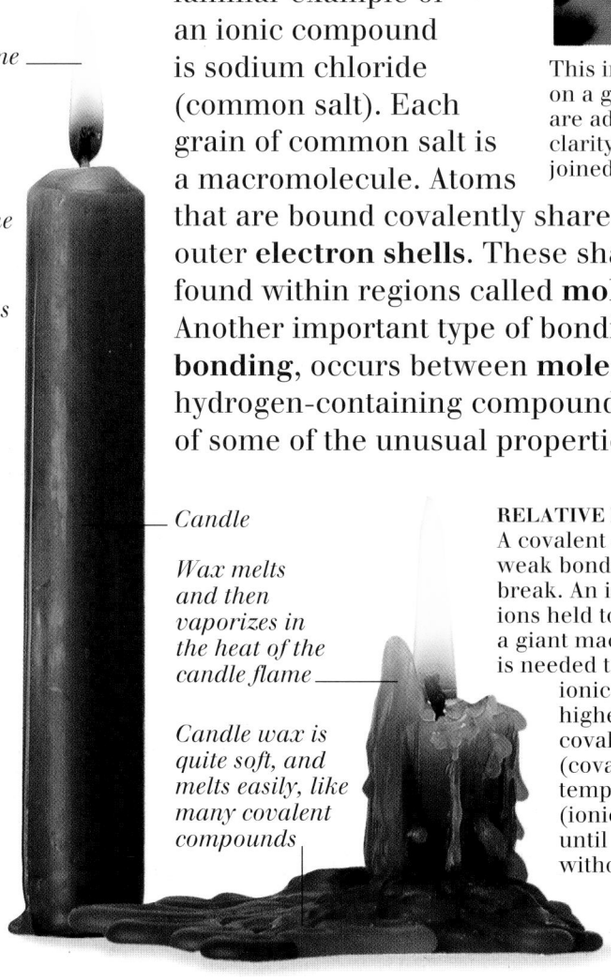

CANDLE WAX, A COVALENT COMPOUND

RELATIVE MELTING POINTS

A covalent compound melts when the weak bonds between its molecules break. An ionic substance consists of ions held together by strong bonds in a giant macromolecule. More **energy** is needed to break these bonds, so ionic substances generally have higher melting points than covalent ones. Candle wax (covalent) melts at a lower temperature than a gas mantle (ionic), which can be heated until it glows white hot without melting.

AN EXAMPLE OF IONIC BONDING

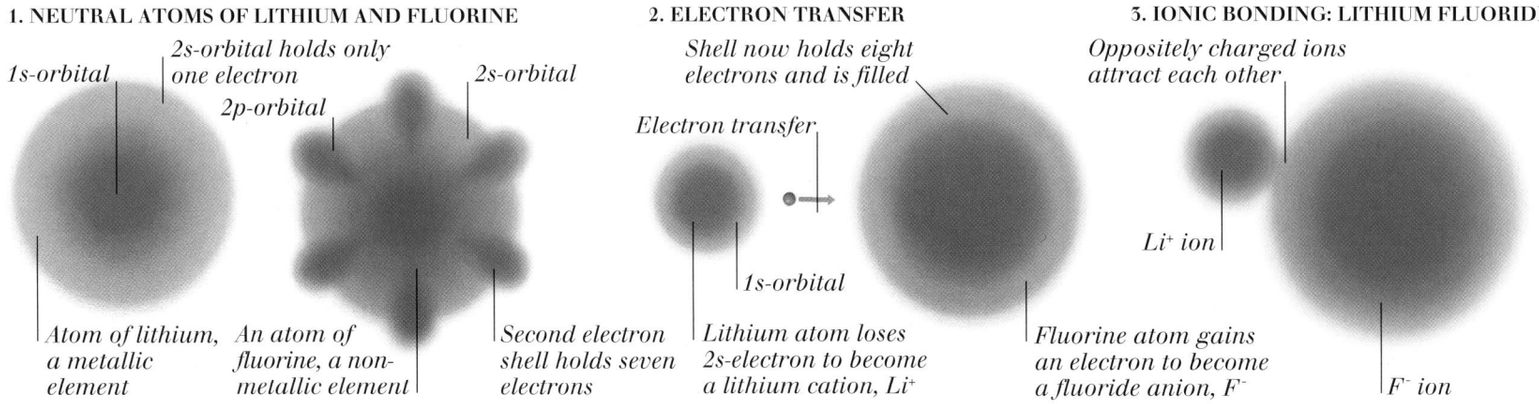

SHERWOOD BRANCH LIBRARY

MOLECULAR ORBITALS

The outer electron **orbitals** (see pp. 10–11) of atoms can overlap to form molecular orbitals, which make the covalent bond. Sometimes, s- and p-orbitals of an atom form combined orbitals, called **hybrid orbitals**, prior to forming molecular orbitals.

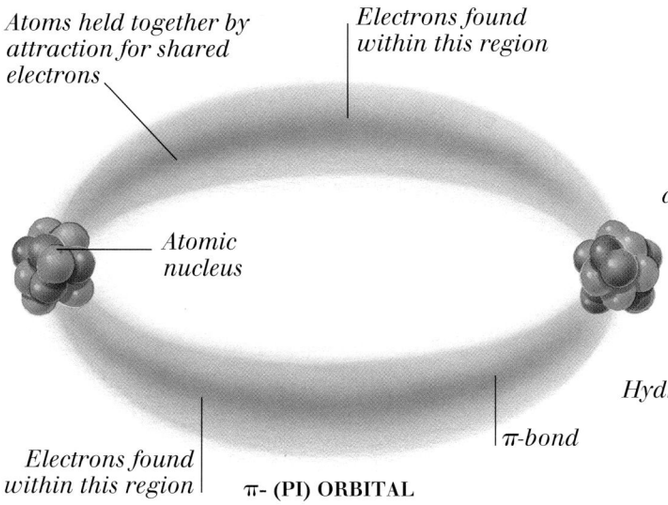

π- (PI) ORBITAL

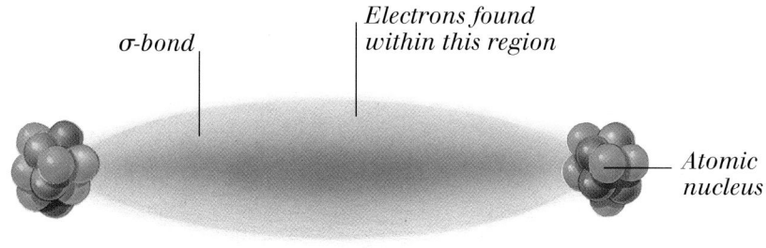

σ- (SIGMA) ORBITAL

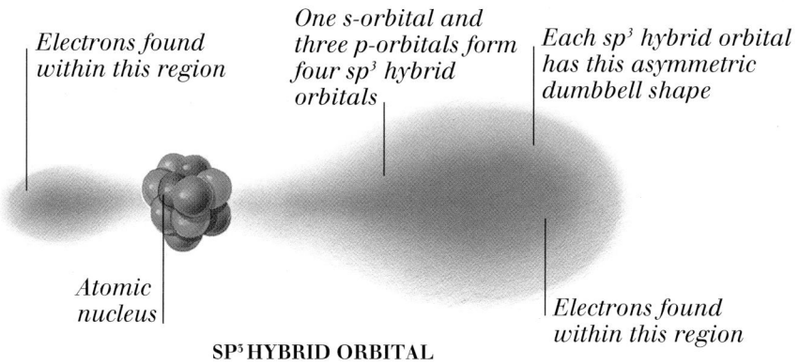

SP³ HYBRID ORBITAL

HYDROGEN BONDING

Hydrogen bonds occur between some hydrogen-containing molecules, such as water. In water molecules, negatively charged electrons are concentrated around the oxygen atom, making it slightly negatively charged relative to the hydrogen atoms. Oppositely charged parts of neighboring molecules attract each other, forming hydrogen bonds.

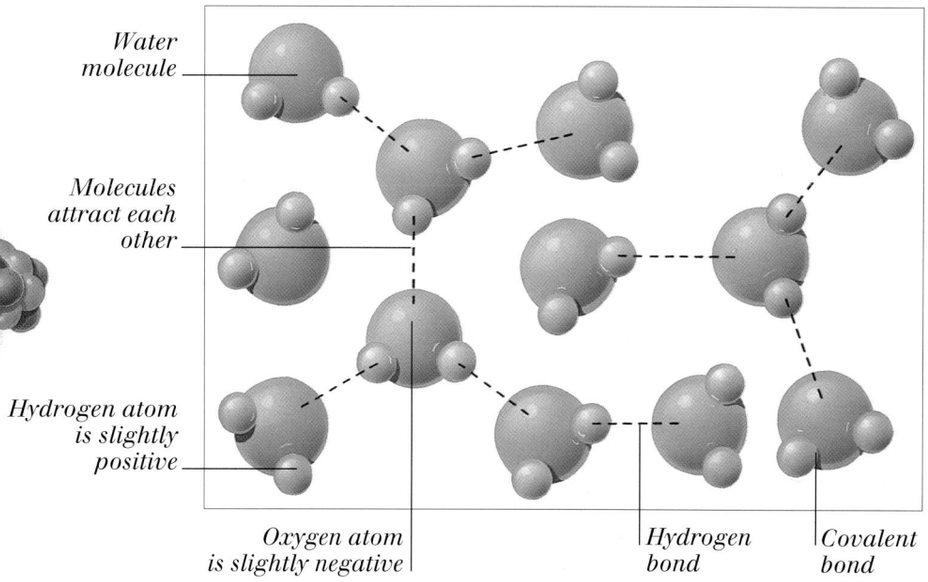

SODIUM CHLORIDE

A macromolecule of sodium chloride forms when sodium **cations** and chloride **anions** bond together. Ions are arranged in the macromolecule in a regular pattern, forming a **crystal**.

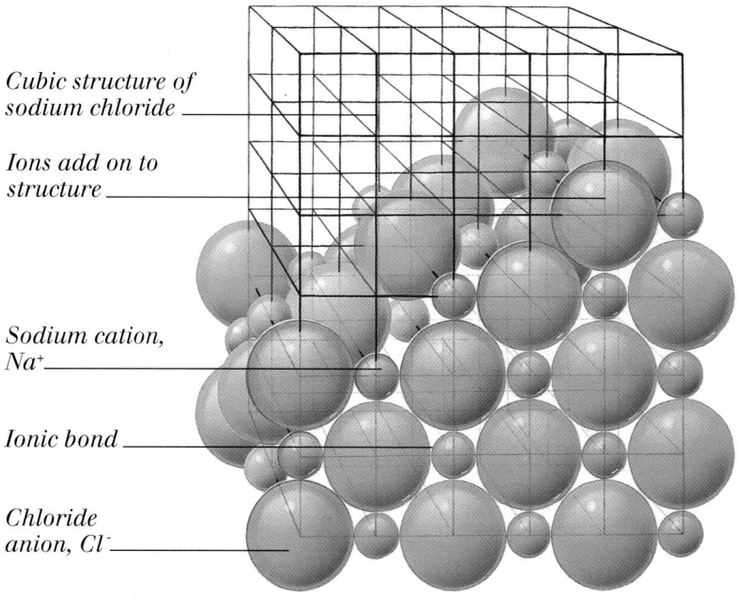

SODIUM CHLORIDE MACROMOLECULE

AN EXAMPLE OF COVALENT BONDING

1. NEUTRAL ATOMS OF HYDROGEN AND FLUORINE

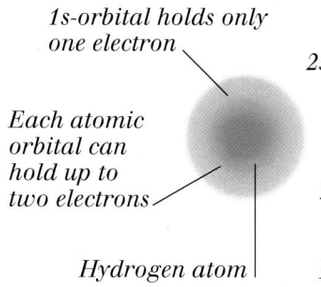

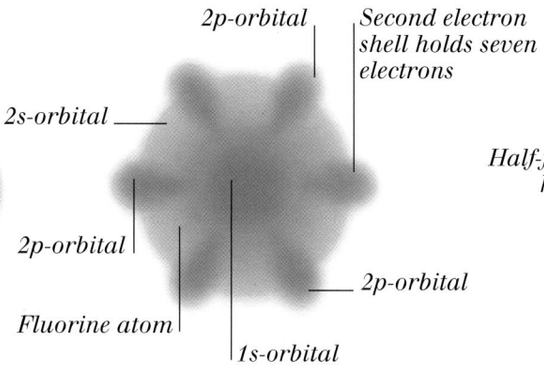

2. HYDROGEN FLUORIDE MOLECULE

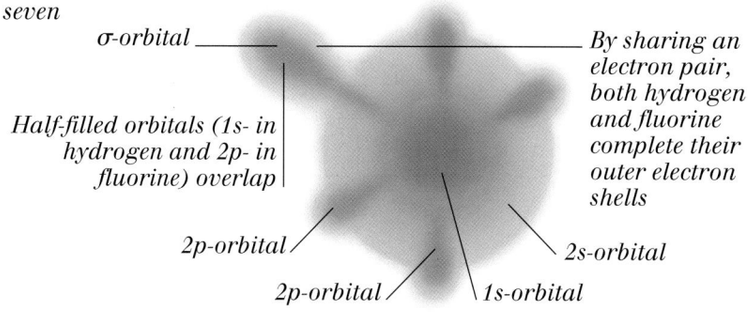

Chemical reactions

IN A CHEMICAL REACTION, THE ATOMS or **ions** of the **reactants** are rearranged to give **products** with different chemical and physical properties. For example, **solutions** of lead nitrate and potassium iodide react to produce a solid **precipitate**. Many reactions are **reversible**. Brown nitrogen dioxide gas **decomposes** at high **temperatures** to form a colorless **mixture** of oxygen and nitrogen monoxide. As the mixture cools, nitrogen dioxide forms again. The reactants and products are said to be in an **equilibrium**, the position of which depends on the temperature. Reactant and product **concentrations** may also affect the equilibrium. **Reaction rates** depend upon a number of factors, including temperature and concentration. Marble and dilute **acid** react together more rapidly if the marble is powdered to give it a greater surface area. During a **chemical reaction**, matter is neither created nor destroyed, only changed from one form to another – so the total mass of the products always equals the mass of the reactants.

Glass bottle

Lead nitrate solution

Funnel

Round-bottomed flask

Conical flask

Potassium iodide solution

Yellow precipitate of lead iodide

DOUBLE DECOMPOSITION REACTION

The reaction between solutions of lead nitrate and potassium iodide is an example of a **double decomposition** reaction. The iodide ions react with the lead ions to form a solid yellow precipitate, while potassium nitrate is left in solution. One metal **cation** of a cation-**anion** pair has been exchanged for the other metal cation.

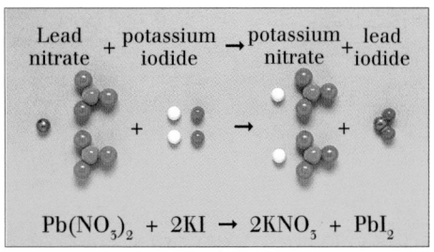

MOLECULAR VIEW
In a double decomposition reaction, the metal cations in solution "swap partners." The lead ions bond to the iodide ions, while the potassium ions associate with the nitrate ions in solution.

EQUILIBRIUM AFFECTED BY TEMPERATURE

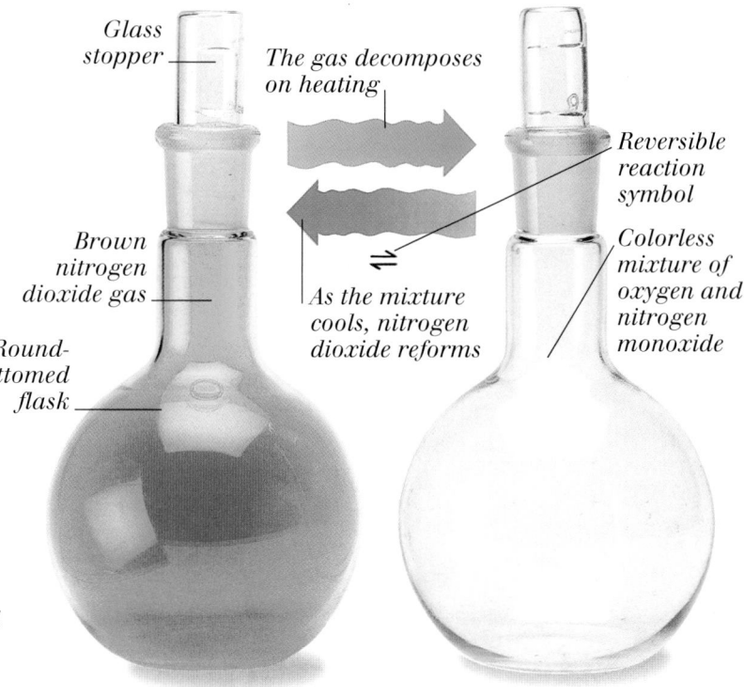

NITROGEN DIOXIDE, NITROGEN MONOXIDE, AND OXYGEN
The flask on the left contains nitrogen dioxide gas. At temperatures above 140°C (284°F), the gas begins to decompose, forming oxygen and nitrogen monoxide. Below this temperature, the equilibrium is pushed the other way and the reaction is reversed.

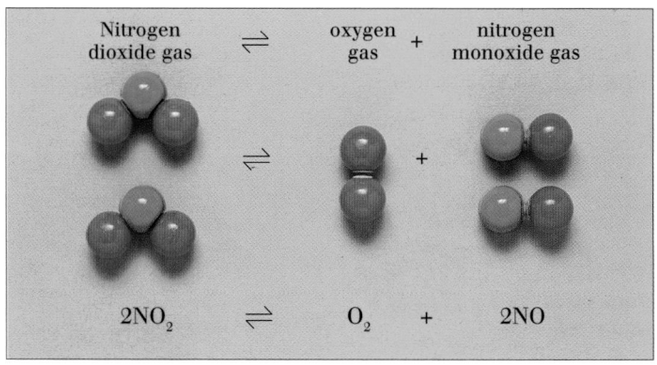

MOLECULAR VIEW
Nitrogen dioxide **molecules** are in equilibrium with **diatomic** molecules of oxygen and nitrogen monoxide.

EQUILIBRIUM AFFECTED BY CONCENTRATION

COBALT AND CHLORIDE IONS
A pink solution of a cobalt(II) **salt** contains cobalt ions, Co^{2+}. When concentrated hydrochloric acid is added to the solution, chloride ions, Cl^-, cluster around the cobalt ions, forming a **complex ion**, $CoCl_4^{2-}$, in a reversible reaction. The presence of this ion gives the solution a blue color. Adding more acid pushes the equilibrium position over toward the product – the complex ion. If the concentration of chloride ions is reduced by adding water, the pink color returns. The addition of water pushes the equilibrium position back toward the reactants – the simple cobalt(II) and chloride ions.

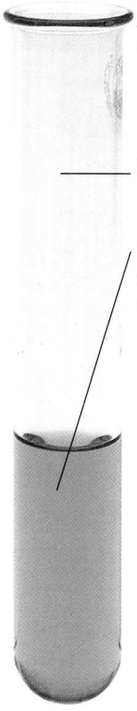

COBALT(II) SALT SOLUTION

ADDITION OF ACID

COMPLEX ION SOLUTION

ADDITION OF WATER

RATE OF REACTION

MARBLE CHIPS
Marble is one form of the **ionic** compound, calcium carbonate, $CaCO_3$. Relatively few of the ions making up large chips of marble (below) are found on the chip surfaces – most of the ions are within the chips.

SURFACE AREA OF REACTANT
When dilute sulfuric acid reacts with marble (right), carbon dioxide gas is produced. If powdered marble is used (far right), more ions come into contact with the acid, and the reaction proceeds more rapidly.

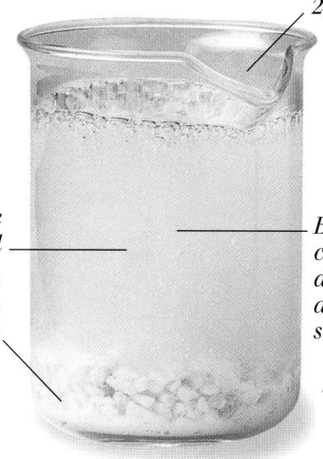

BEAKER WITH CHIPS

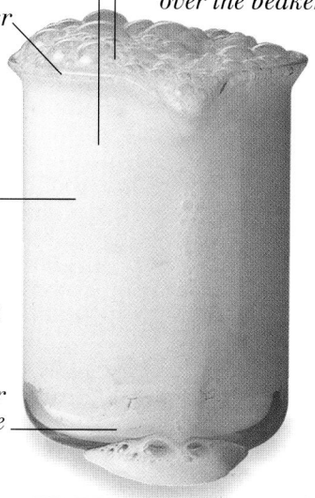

BEAKER WITH POWDER

CONSERVATION OF MASS

In every chemical reaction, mass is conserved. The reaction below is carried out in a sealed flask to prevent the escape of the gaseous product. An accurate chemical balance shows that there is no gain or loss of mass.

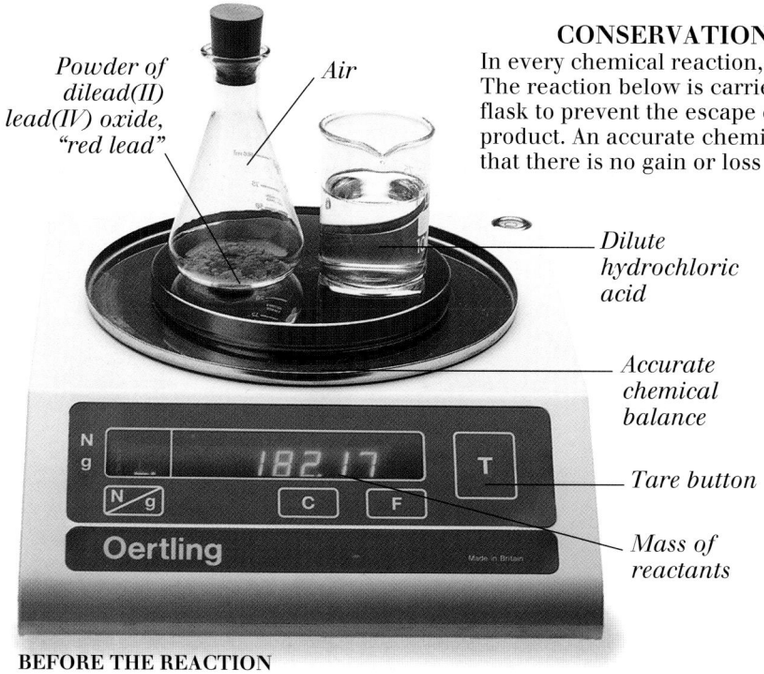

BEFORE THE REACTION
The reactants are weighed before the reaction. The balance is tared (or zeroed) with just the glassware, so that only the mass of the substances inside the glassware will be displayed.

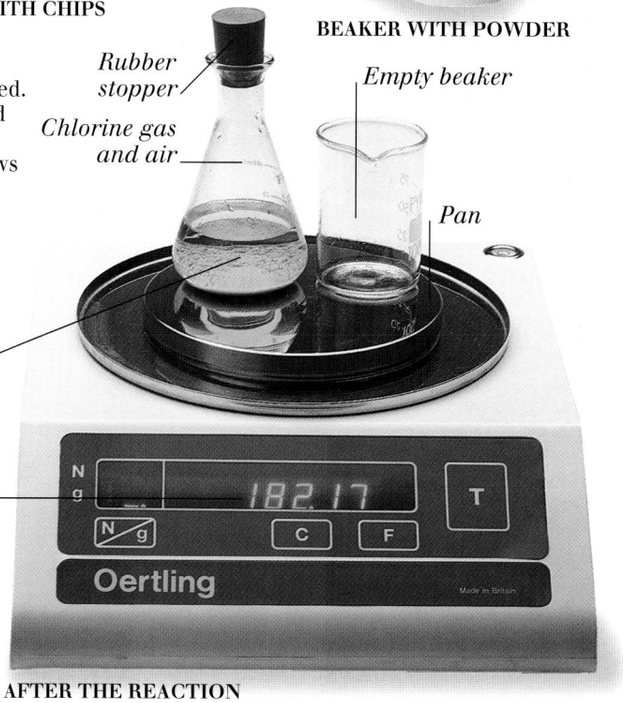

AFTER THE REACTION
The reactants are mixed in the conical flask, and the flask is quickly sealed so that no reaction products can escape. The mass of products is identical to the mass of reactants.

Oxidation and reduction

IN MANY CHEMICAL REACTIONS (see pp. 18–19), **electrons** are transferred between the **atoms** or **ions** taking part. For example, when nitric acid reacts with copper metal, copper atoms lose electrons to become Cu^{2+} ions, while the acid gains electrons. An atom or ion that loses electrons (or gains oxygen) is said to undergo **oxidation**, while an atom or ion that gains electrons (or loses oxygen) undergoes **reduction**. Reactions that involve oxidation and reduction are called **redox reactions**. When an atom or ion is oxidized or reduced, its **oxidation number** changes by the number of electrons transferred. The oxidation number of any atom is 0 (zero), while that of an **element** in a **compound** is given by Roman numerals or by the amount of charge on its ions. For example, iron exists as iron(II) ions, Fe^{2+}, in rust, where it has an oxidation number of +2. An older definition of oxidation was combination with oxygen, as happens in **burning** reactions.

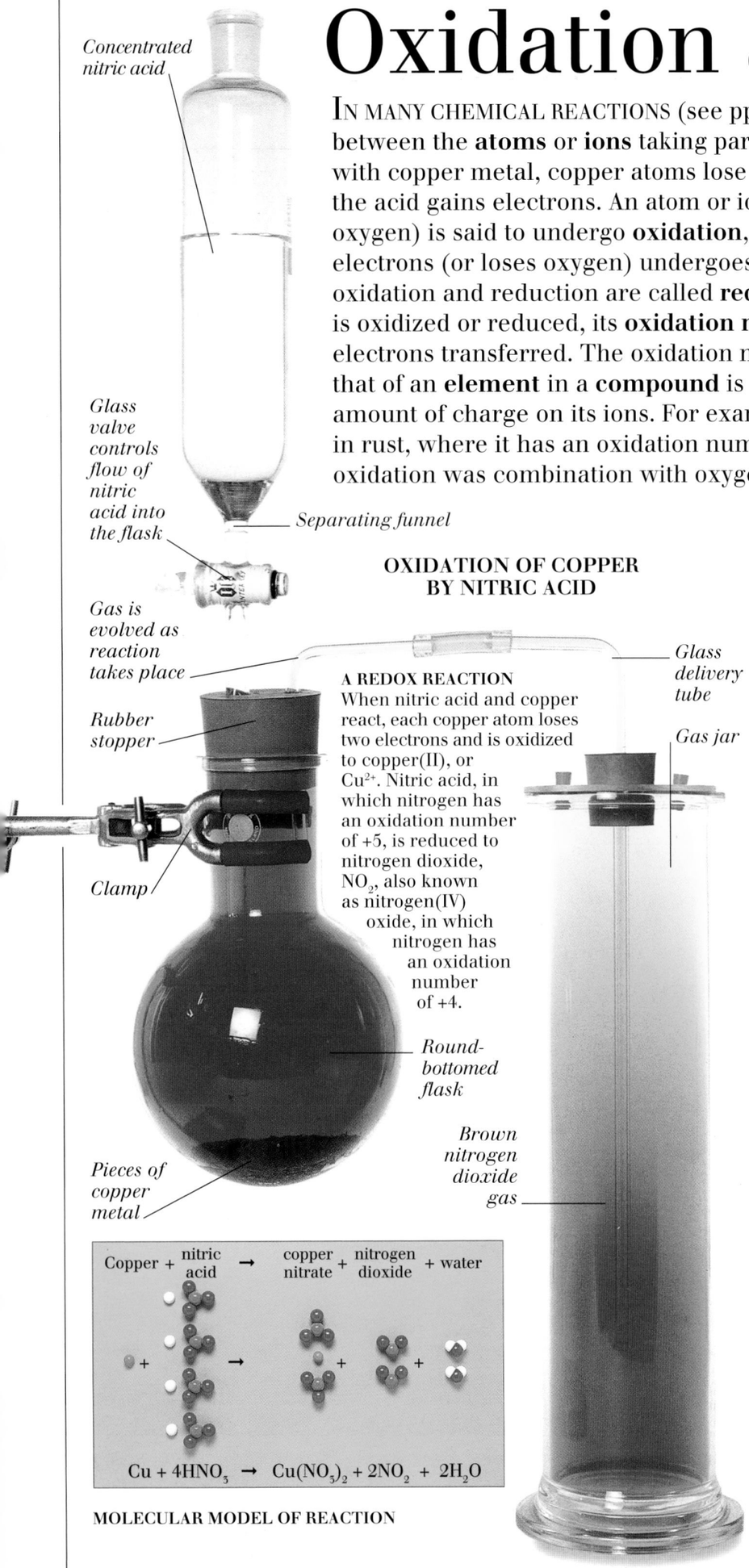

OXIDATION OF COPPER BY NITRIC ACID

A REDOX REACTION
When nitric acid and copper react, each copper atom loses two electrons and is oxidized to copper(II), or Cu^{2+}. Nitric acid, in which nitrogen has an oxidation number of +5, is reduced to nitrogen dioxide, NO_2, also known as nitrogen(IV) oxide, in which nitrogen has an oxidation number of +4.

MOLECULAR MODEL OF REACTION

RUSTING OF IRON
The rusting of iron is an example of a redox reaction. Iron is oxidized to iron(II), with an oxidation number of +2, when it reacts with water and oxygen. The resulting compound, known as rust, is hydrated iron oxide. The tubes below show that both water and oxygen are needed for rust to form.

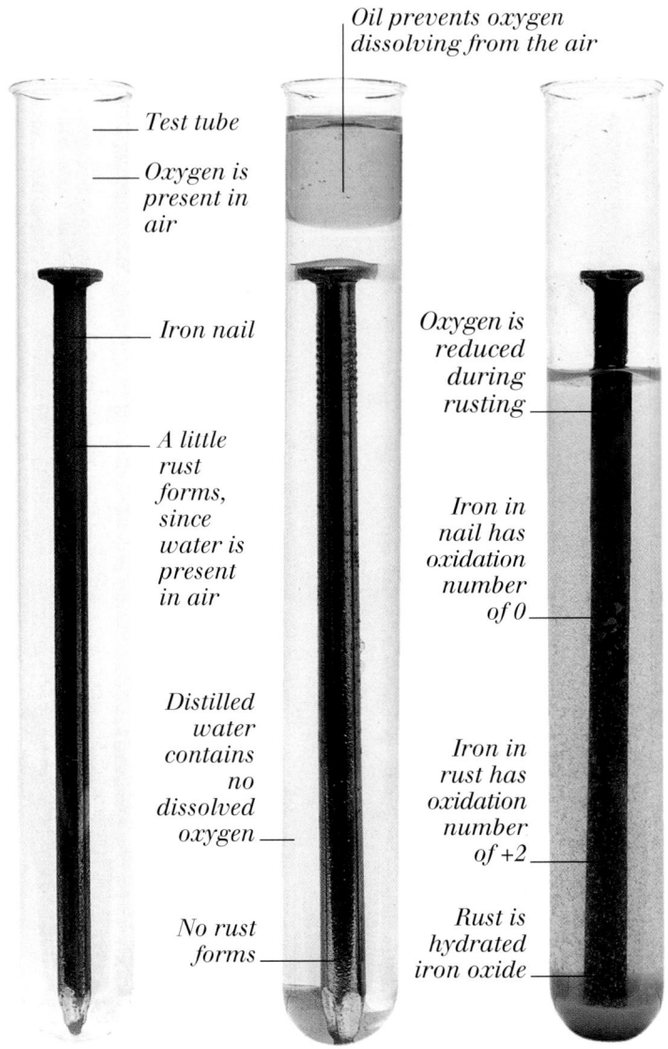

AIR, NO WATER — WATER, NO AIR — AIR AND WATER

COMBUSTION REACTION

All combustion reactions are redox reactions. Combustion, or burning, is defined as the rapid **exothermic** combination of a substance with oxygen. Candle wax is a **mixture** of **hydrocarbons**, mainly the **alkane** $C_{18}H_{38}$. Oxygen combines with the carbon atoms present to form carbon dioxide, and with the hydrogen atoms to form water.

Thistle funnel traps gases that are products of the reaction

Carbon and hydrogen are oxidized to carbon dioxide gas and water respectively

Delivery tube

Water droplets form as the vapor condenses

Clamp stand

TESTING FOR THE PRODUCTS
Anhydrous copper sulfate (see pp. 30–31) indicates the presence of water. The presence of carbon dioxide is indicated by limewater (see pp. 54–55).

Unburned carbon collects as soot

Rubber stopper

Rubber stopper

Combustion releases heat, causing unburned wax to glow in a flame

Products of reaction drawn through the glassware by pump

Near the flame, the wax vaporizes and combines with oxygen

Clamp

Side arm test tube

Wick

Glass U-tube

To pump

Wax candle consists of hydrocarbons

Limewater (calcium hydroxide solution)

Anhydrous copper(II) sulfate turns blue, indicating the presence of water

Limewater turns milky, indicating the presence of carbon dioxide

OXIDATION AS TRANSFER OF ELECTRONS

In many redox reactions, electrons are physically transferred from one atom to another, as shown.

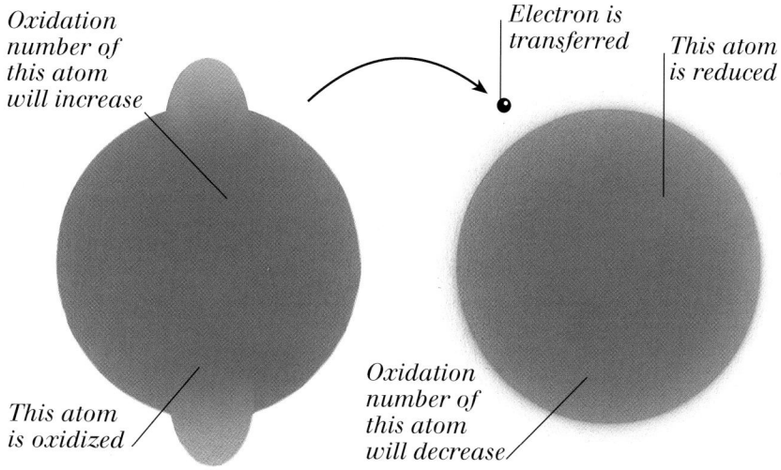

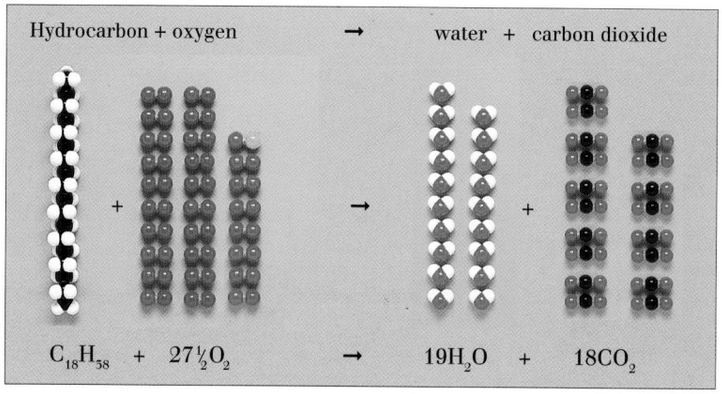

MOLECULAR MODEL OF REACTION
Two **molecules** of the hydrocarbon $C_{18}H_{38}$ react with 55 oxygen molecules, producing 38 molecules of water and 36 of carbon dioxide. Half of these amounts have been shown above.

Acids and bases

ACID IS A COMMON WORD in everyday use, but it has a precise definition in chemistry. An **acid** is defined as a **molecule** or an **ion** that can donate **protons**, or hydrogen ions, H^+. A **base** is a substance, often an oxide or hydroxide, that accepts protons, and an **alkali** is a base that is water-soluble. Some substances, such as water, can act as either acids or bases, depending on the other substances present. Acids and bases undergo characteristic reactions together, usually in **aqueous solution**, producing a **salt** (see pp. 24–25) and water. In **solution**, acid-base reactions involve the transfer of **hydronium ions** or hydrated protons, H_3O^+. These ions form, for example, when hydrogen chloride gas dissolves in water. The **pH scale** gives the **concentration** of hydronium ions in solution. As pH falls below 7, a solution becomes more acidic. Conversely, as pH rises above 7, the solution becomes more alkaline. The pH of a solution can be estimated using pigments called **indicators**, or measured accurately with a pH meter.

UNIVERSAL INDICATOR PAPER

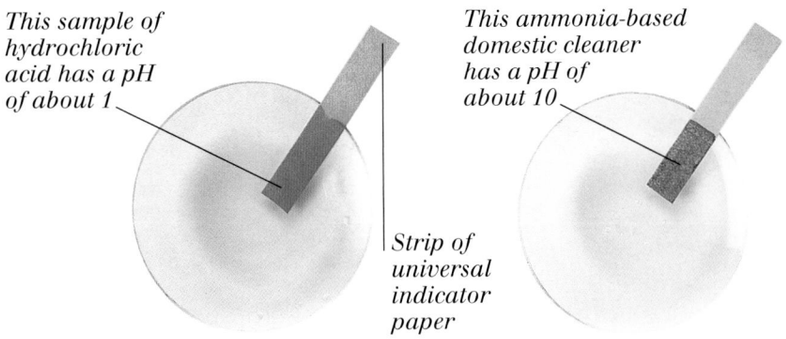

HYDROCHLORIC ACID

DOMESTIC CLEANER

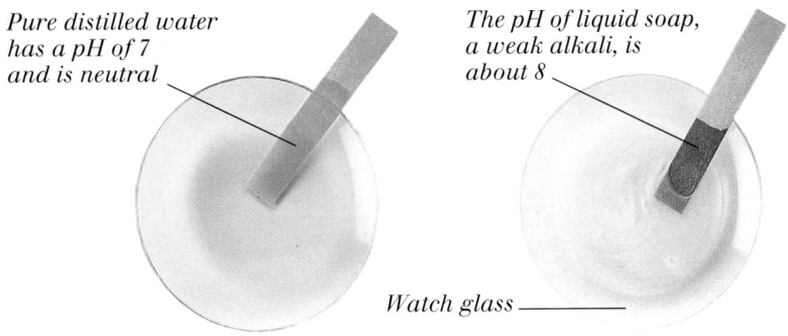

DISTILLED WATER

LIQUID SOAP

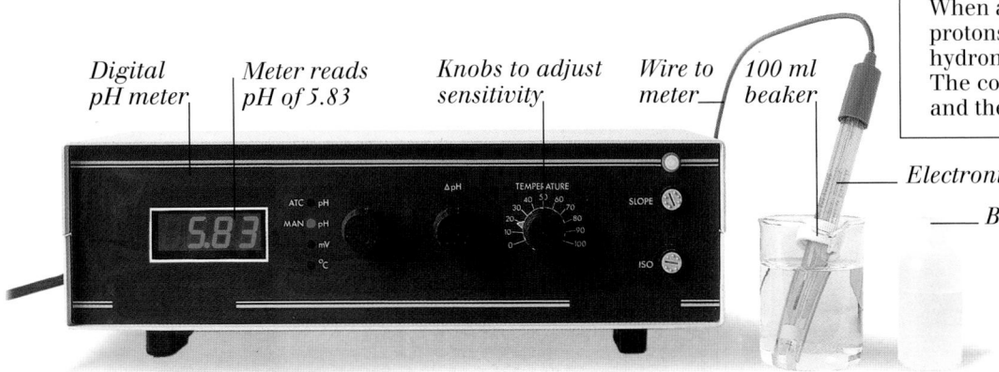

MEASURING pH
This digital pH meter accurately measures hydronium ion concentration. Such meters are often used to find the pH of colored solutions, which could mask the true color of indicators.

THE MEANING OF pH

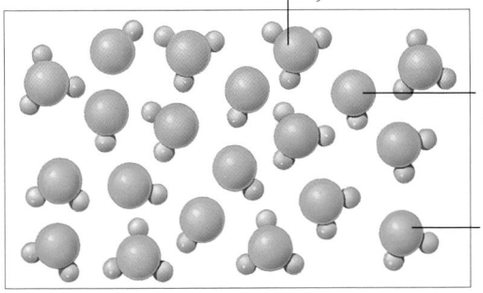

PURE WATER (NEUTRAL)
Some of the molecules of liquid water break up, or dissociate, forming hydroxide ions, OH^-, and hydrogen ions, H^+, that become hydrated, H_3O^+. In one liter of pure water at 20°C, there are 10^{-7} **moles** (see pp. 10–11) of each type of ion. This gives a pH value of 7 (neutral) for pure water.

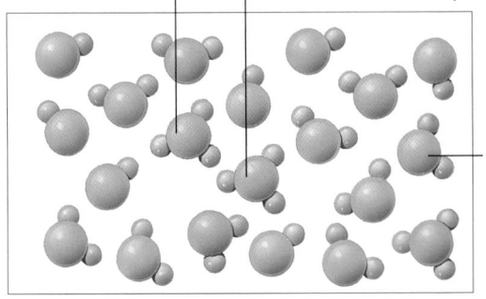

ALKALINE SOLUTION
When an alkali is added to water, it removes protons, H^+, from some of the hydronium ions, H_3O^+, present, forming more water molecules. The lower the concentration of H_3O^+, the higher the pH. Typically, a weakly alkaline solution has a pH of 10, and a strongly alkaline solution has a pH of 14.

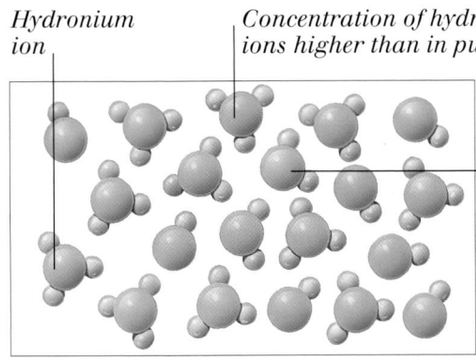

ACIDIC SOLUTION
When an acid is dissolved in water, it donates protons, H^+, to water molecules, H_2O, making more hydronium ions, H_3O^+. Water thus acts as a base. The concentration of hydronium ions increases, and the pH decreases.

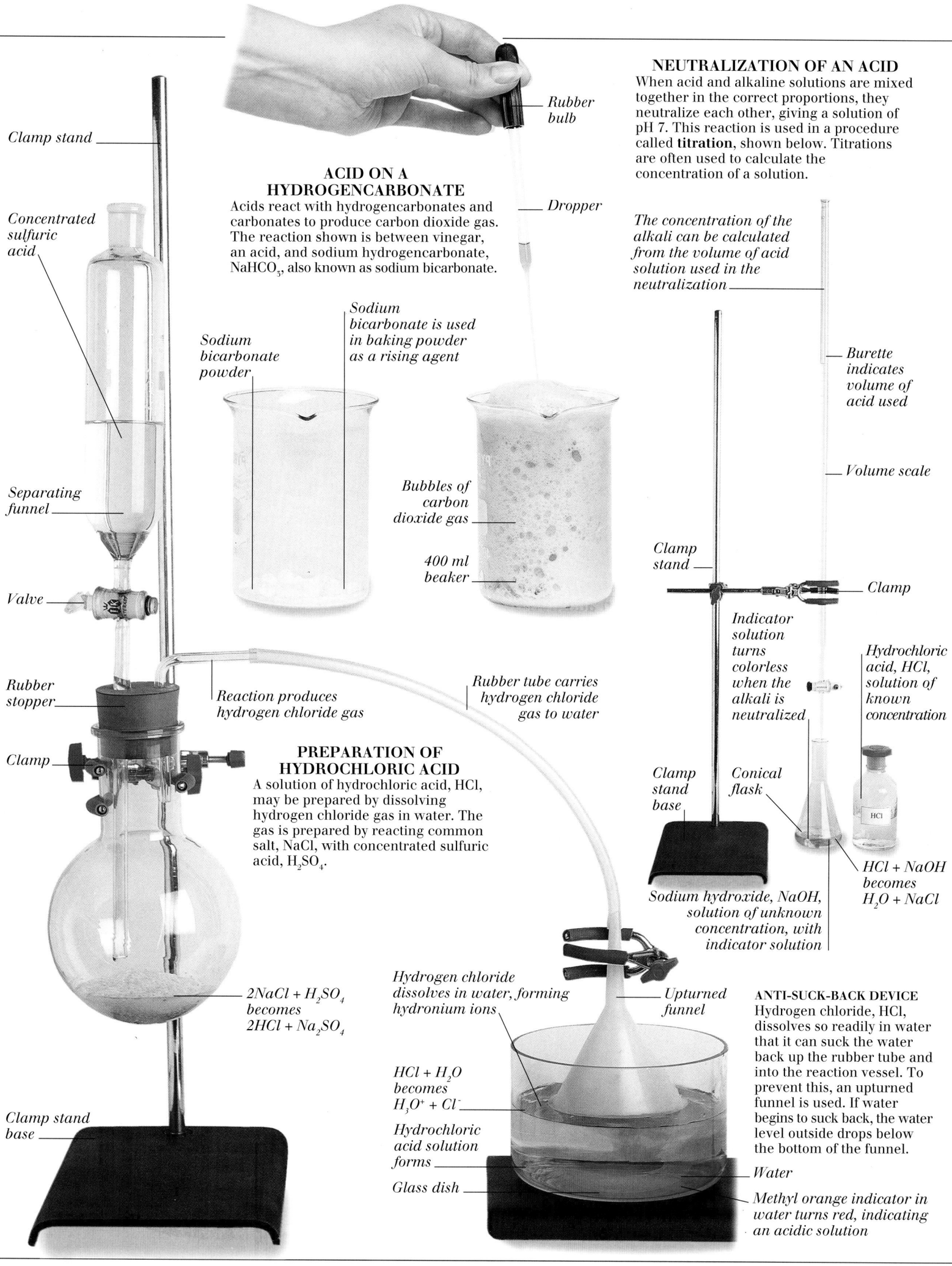

ACID ON A HYDROGENCARBONATE

Acids react with hydrogencarbonates and carbonates to produce carbon dioxide gas. The reaction shown is between vinegar, an acid, and sodium hydrogencarbonate, $NaHCO_3$, also known as sodium bicarbonate.

NEUTRALIZATION OF AN ACID

When acid and alkaline solutions are mixed together in the correct proportions, they neutralize each other, giving a solution of pH 7. This reaction is used in a procedure called **titration**, shown below. Titrations are often used to calculate the concentration of a solution.

PREPARATION OF HYDROCHLORIC ACID

A solution of hydrochloric acid, HCl, may be prepared by dissolving hydrogen chloride gas in water. The gas is prepared by reacting common salt, NaCl, with concentrated sulfuric acid, H_2SO_4.

ANTI-SUCK-BACK DEVICE

Hydrogen chloride, HCl, dissolves so readily in water that it can suck the water back up the rubber tube and into the reaction vessel. To prevent this, an upturned funnel is used. If water begins to suck back, the water level outside drops below the bottom of the funnel.

Salts

WHENEVER AN ACID AND A BASE **neutralize** each other (see pp. 22–23), the **products** of the reaction always include a **salt**. A salt is a **compound** that consists of **cations** (positive **ions**) and **anions** (negative ions). The cation is usually a metal ion, such as the sodium ion, Na^+. The anion can be a nonmetal such as the chloride ion, Cl^-, although more often it is a unit called a **radical**. This is a combination of nonmetals that remains unchanged during most reactions. So, for example, when copper(II) oxide is added to sulfuric acid, the sulfate radical (SO_4^{2-}) becomes associated with copper ions, forming the salt copper(II) sulfate, $CuSO_4$. Salts are very widespread compounds – the most familiar being sodium chloride, or common salt. Mineral water contains salts, which are formed when slightly **acidic** rainwater dissolves rocks such as limestone. Water that contains large amounts of certain dissolved salts is called hard water (see pp. 38–39). A class of salts called acid salts contains a positive hydrogen ion in addition to the usual metal cation. Acid salts can be prepared by careful **titration** of an acid and a **base**.

FORMATION OF SALTS

In the generalized equations below, an acid reacts with three typical bases – a hydroxide, an oxide, and a carbonate. A cation from the base combines with the acid's anion or negative radical, displacing the hydrogen ion to form a salt.

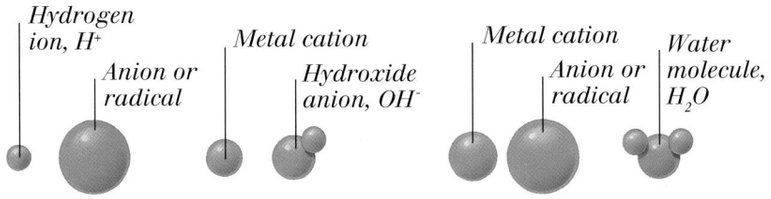

ACID + BASE (HYDROXIDE) → SALT + WATER

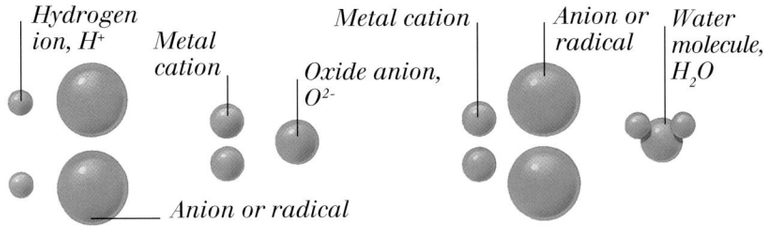

ACID + BASE (OXIDE) → SALT + WATER

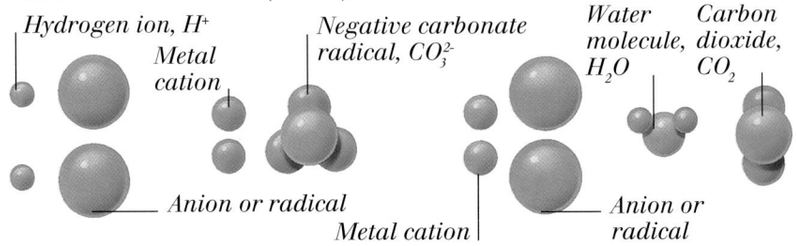

ACID + BASE (CARBONATE) → SALT + WATER + CARBON DIOXIDE

COPPER(II) SULFATE

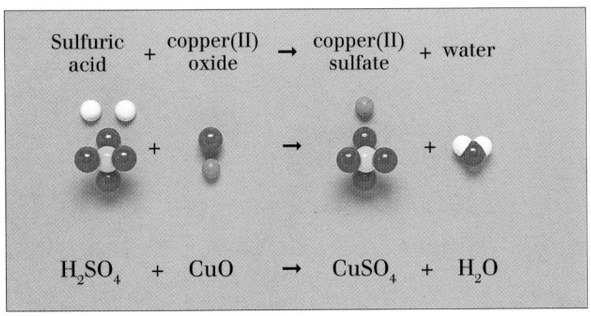

MOLECULAR VIEW

When the base copper(II) oxide reacts with sulfuric acid, copper(II) ions take the place of the hydrogen in the acid. The salt formed is therefore copper(II) sulfate. Water is the other product. The sulfate ion is a radical.

COPPER(II) OXIDE AND SULFURIC ACID

Copper(II) oxide, a black powder, is a base. When added to colorless dilute sulfuric acid, a neutralization reaction occurs. Hydrogen from the acid and oxygen from copper(II) oxide form water, while copper ions and the sulfate radical form the salt copper(II) sulfate.

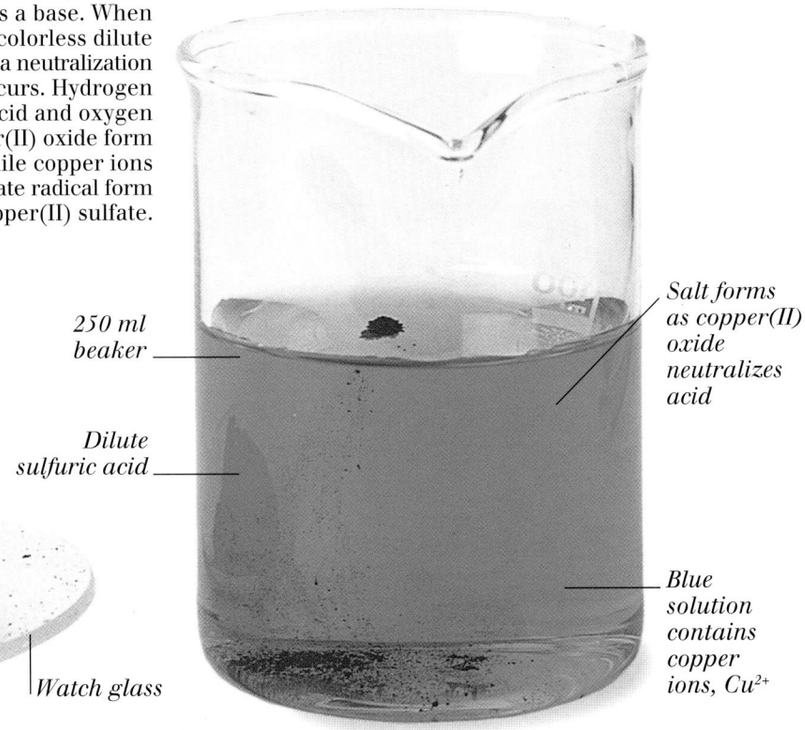

DISSOLVED SALTS IN MINERAL WATER

BOILING MINERAL WATER
Nearly all salts are **ionic**, and dissolve to a certain extent in water. Mineral water contains small amounts of dissolved salts. They are normally invisible, because they exist as individual ions and radicals.

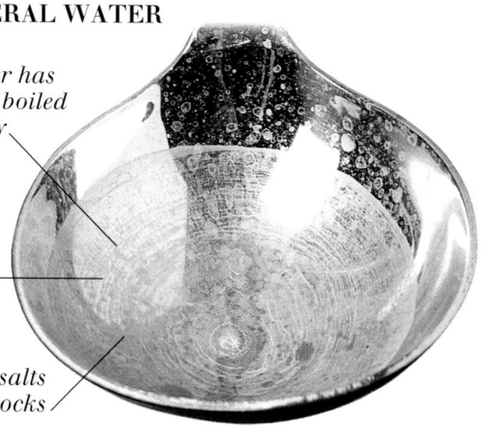

RESIDUE AFTER BOILING
When mineral water is boiled, a small amount of solid residue is formed. This consists of salts. Pure water would leave no residue. The salts in mineral water originate in rocks over which rainwater passes.

ACID ON LIMESTONE

Limestone is one form of calcium carbonate, $CaCO_3$. It dissolves in acid to form a calcium salt. Carbon dioxide is evolved during the reaction, and geologists sometimes use this as a test for a carbonate rock (see pp. 54–55).

ACID SALTS

In an acid salt, only some of the hydrogen ions of the acid are replaced by other cations. Here, sulfuric acid is neutralized by the base sodium hydroxide. The volume of base used is noted. In a separate flask, only half this volume of base is added to the same volume of acid, forming the acid salt sodium hydrogensulfate.

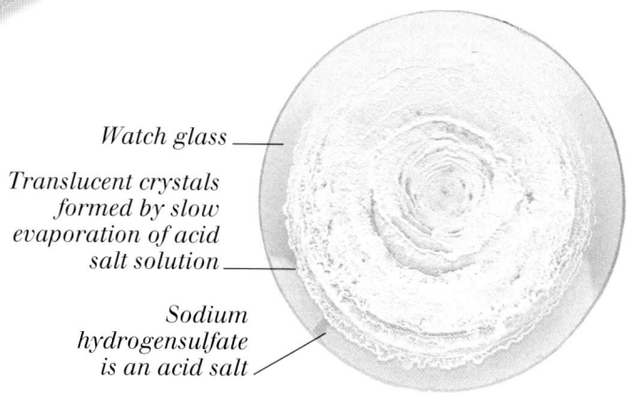

CRYSTALS OF SODIUM HYDROGENSULFATE

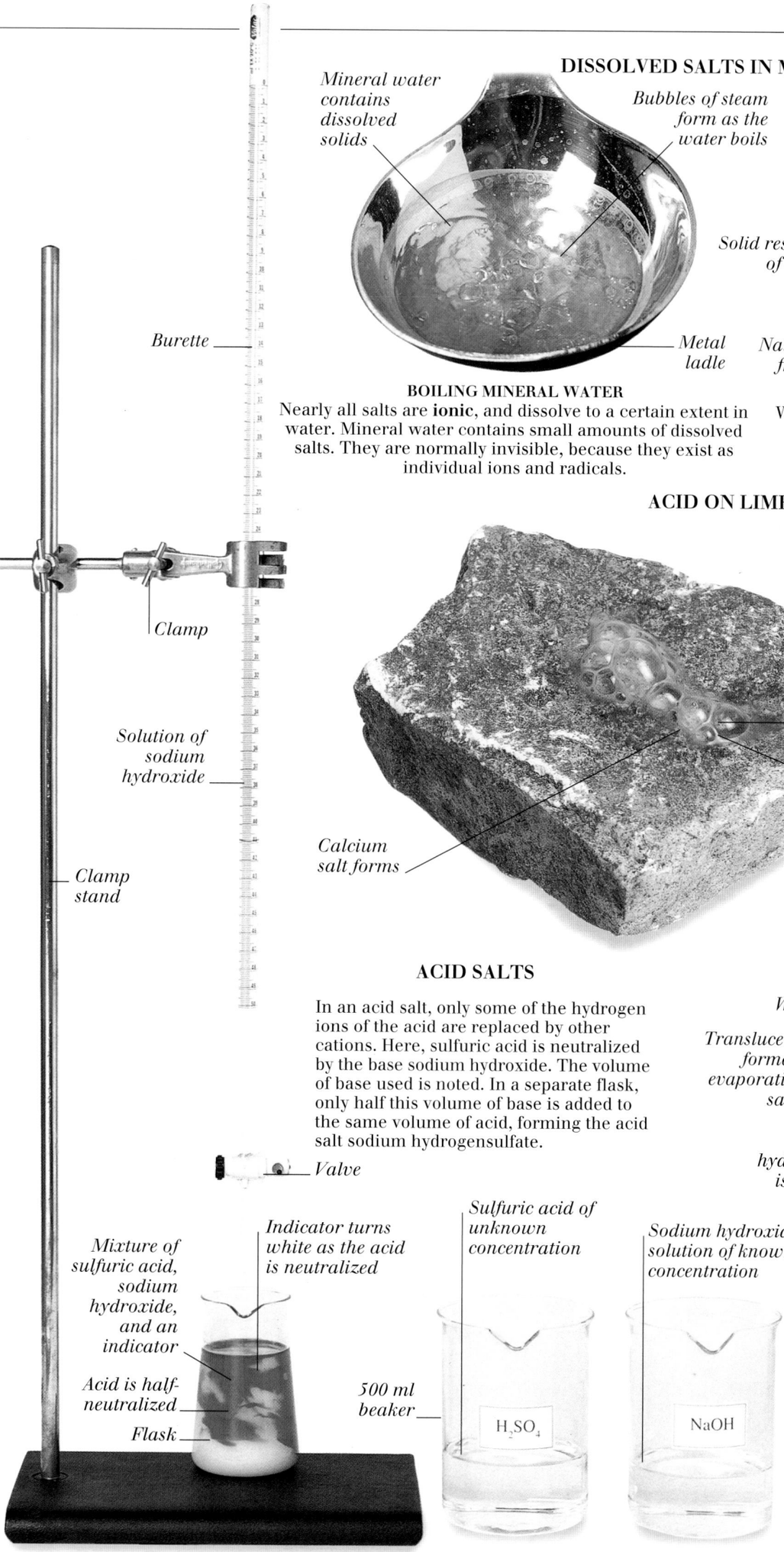

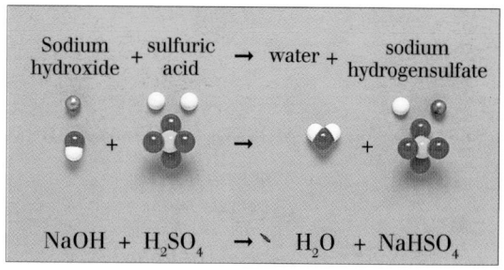

MOLECULAR VIEW
Each unit of sulfuric acid has two hydrogen ions. Adding the right amount of sodium hydroxide removes only one of these ions.

Catalysts

A CATALYST IS A SUBSTANCE that increases the **rate** at which a reaction takes place but is unchanged itself at the end of the reaction. Certain **catalysts** are used up in one stage of a reaction and regenerated at a later stage. Light is sometimes considered to be a catalyst – although it is not a substance – because it speeds up certain reactions. This process is referred to as photocatalysis, and is very important in photography and in **photosynthesis** (see pp. 38–39). Often, catalysts simply provide a suitable surface upon which the reaction can take place. Such surface catalysis often involves **transition metals**, such as iron or nickel. Surface catalysis occurs in catalytic converters in automobiles, which speed up reactions that change harmful pollutant gases into less harmful ones. **Enzymes** are biological catalysts and are nearly all **proteins**. They catalyze reactions in living organisms. For example, an enzyme called ptyalin in saliva helps to digest or break down starch in food to make sugars that can be readily absorbed by the body. Enzymes are also important in turning sugar into alcohol during fermentation.

PHOTOCATALYSIS

Light can promote, or speed up, a reaction. Here, both tubes contain a yellow **precipitate** of silver bromide (see pp. 54–55). For a period of about ten minutes, one of the tubes has been left in a dark cupboard while the other has been left in the light. The light has caused silver **ions** to become **atoms** of silver. Photographic films contain tiny granules of silver halides, which produce silver on the negative wherever it is hit by light.

Test tube

Precipitate of silver bromide

Only slight brown color

The reaction proceeds more slowly in the absence of light

Precipitate of silver bromide has turned black-brown

Test tube

Light speeds up reaction

Black-brown color caused by silver metal

Bromine produced by reaction dissolves in water

Silver bromide precipitate → bromine gas + silver metal

$2AgBr \rightarrow Br_2 + 2Ag$

MOLECULAR VIEW OF REACTION

TUBE LEFT IN DARKNESS

TUBE LEFT IN LIGHT

CATALYSIS AT A SURFACE

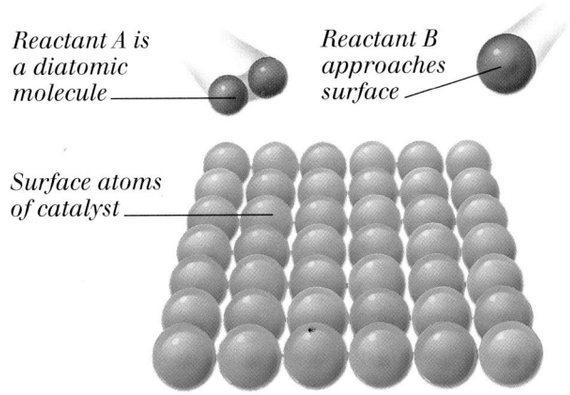

REACTANTS APPROACH SURFACE
In this reaction, one of the **reactants** is a **diatomic molecule** that must be split before it will react.

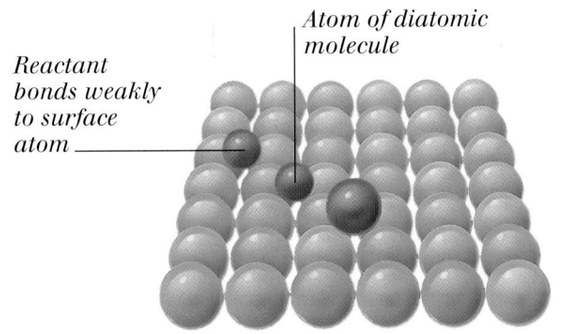

REACTANTS BOND TO SURFACE
The reactants form weak bonds with the surface atoms. As the diatomic molecule bonds, it breaks into two individual atoms.

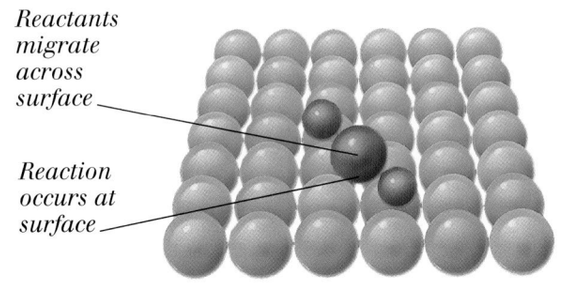

REACTION TAKES PLACE
The reactants move, or migrate, across the surface. When they meet, the reaction takes place. The surface is unchanged.

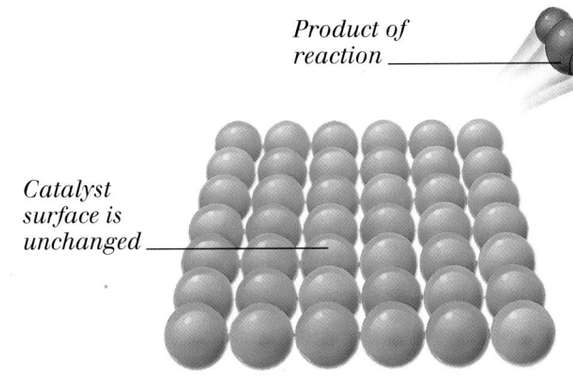

PRODUCT LEAVES SURFACE
The reaction **product** leaves the surface, to which it was very weakly bonded, and the reaction is complete.

EXAMPLES OF SURFACE CATALYSTS

CATALYTIC CONVERTER
Many automobiles are fitted with a catalytic converter, as part of the exhaust system. Inside is a fine honeycomb structure coated with catalysts. Harmful carbon monoxide, nitrogen oxides, and unburned **hydrocarbons** are converted into carbon dioxide and harmless water and nitrogen.

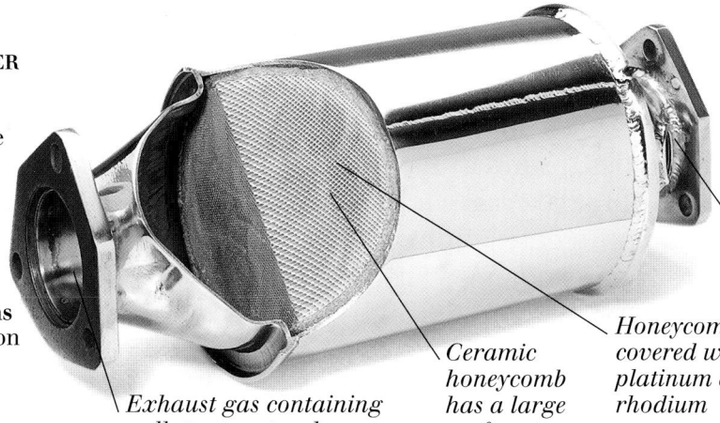

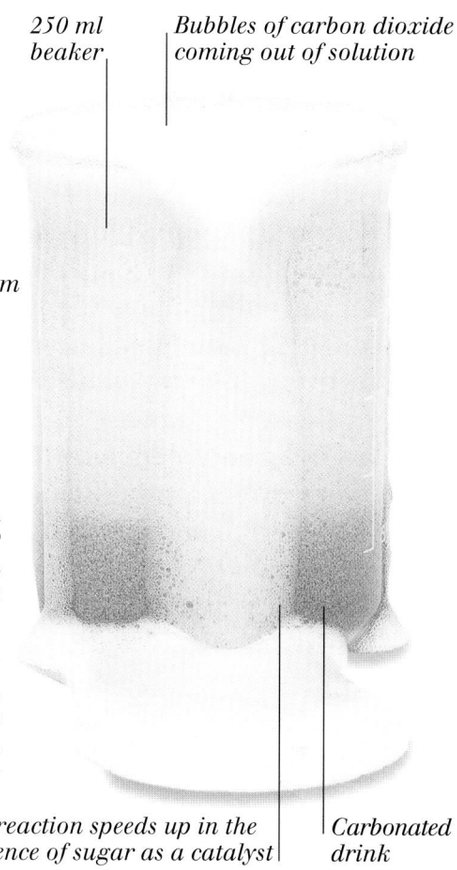

SUGAR AS A SURFACE CATALYST
Carbonated drinks contain carbon dioxide gas dissolved in water. The carbon dioxide normally comes out of **solution** quite slowly. This reaction speeds up at a catalytic surface, such as that of sugar.

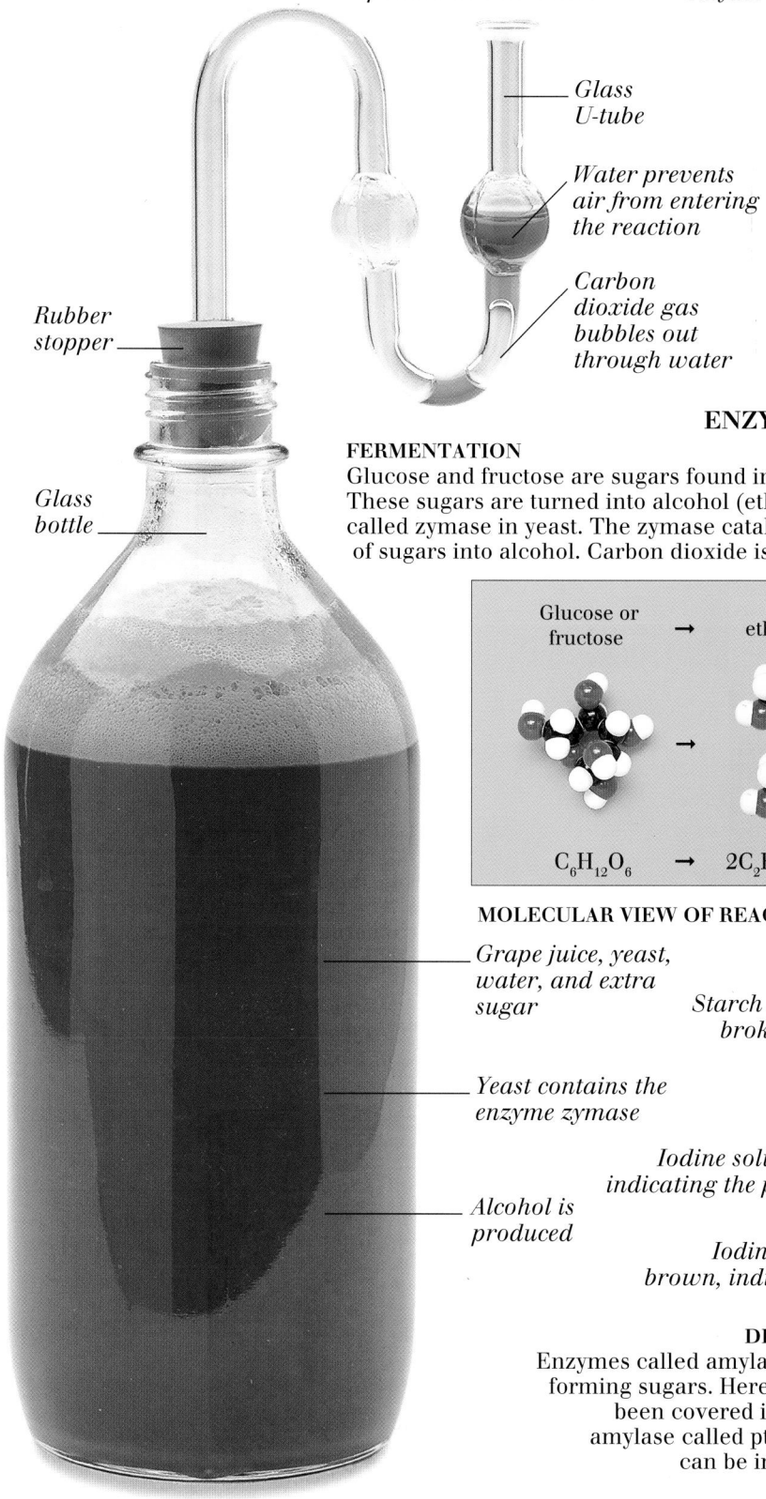

ENZYMES

FERMENTATION
Glucose and fructose are sugars found in fruit such as grapes. These sugars are turned into alcohol (ethanol) by an enzyme called zymase in yeast. The zymase catalyzes the **decomposition** of sugars into alcohol. Carbon dioxide is also produced.

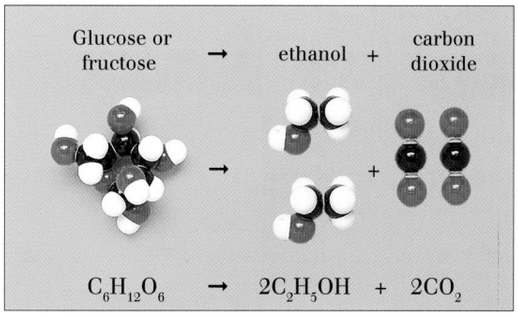

MOLECULAR VIEW OF REACTION

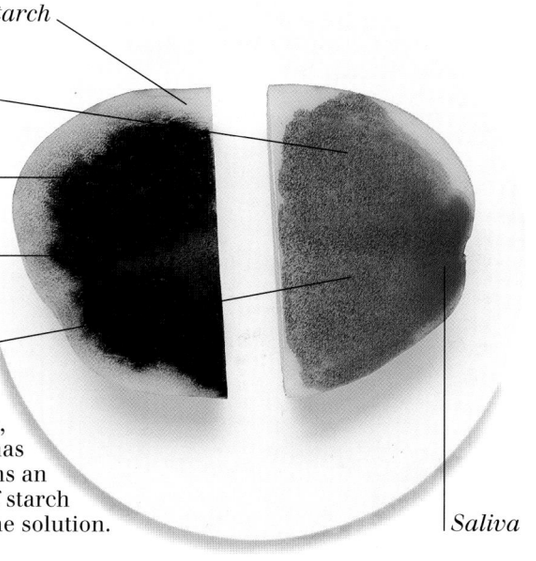

POWDERED LAUNDRY DETERGENTS
Some powdered laundry detergents contain enzymes, which catalyze the breakdown of proteins that make up stains in clothing. The enzymes are denatured, or damaged, at high **temperatures**, so these detergents only work at low temperatures.

DIGESTION OF STARCH
Enzymes called amylases break down starch, forming sugars. Here, one side of a potato has been covered in saliva, which contains an amylase called ptyalin. The presence of starch can be indicated using an iodine solution.

Heat in chemistry

HEAT IS A FORM OF ENERGY that a substance possesses due to the movement or vibration of its **atoms**, **molecules**, or **ions**. The **temperature** of a substance is a measure of the average heat (or **kinetic**) **energy** of its particles, and is a factor in determining whether the substance is solid, liquid, or gas. Energy changes are involved in all reactions. For example, light energy (see pp. 38–39) and electrical energy (see pp. 34–35) can make reactions occur or can be released as a result of reactions. Heat energy is taken in or released by most reactions. Some reactions, such as the **burning** of wood, need an initial input of energy, called **activation energy**, in order for them to occur. Once established, however, the burning reaction releases heat energy to the surroundings – it is an **exothermic** reaction. Other reactions take heat from their surroundings, and are called **endothermic** reactions. The thermite reaction, in which aluminum metal reacts with a metal oxide, is so exothermic that the heat released can be used to weld metals.

LIQUID CHLORINE

A gas becomes a liquid if cooled below its boiling point. Here, chlorine gas has been pumped into a test tube. Heat energy is then removed from the gas by cooling the tube in dry ice.

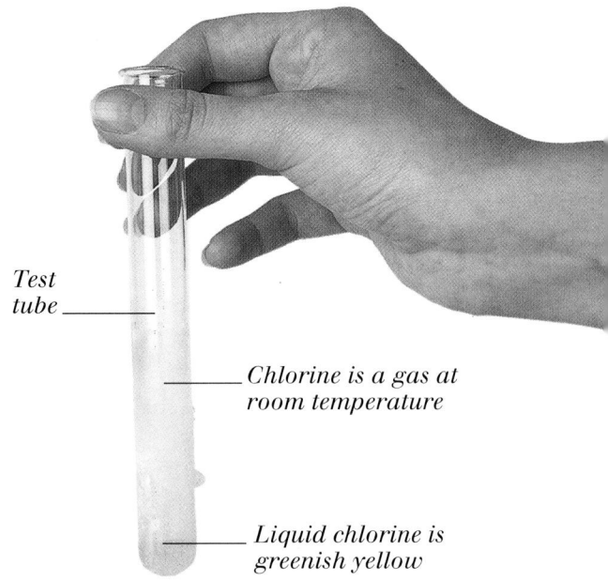

ACTIVATION ENERGY

Friction between a match head and a rough surface produces heat. This heat provides the energy that the chemicals in the match head need to start reacting. The heat released in this reaction begins the burning of the wood.

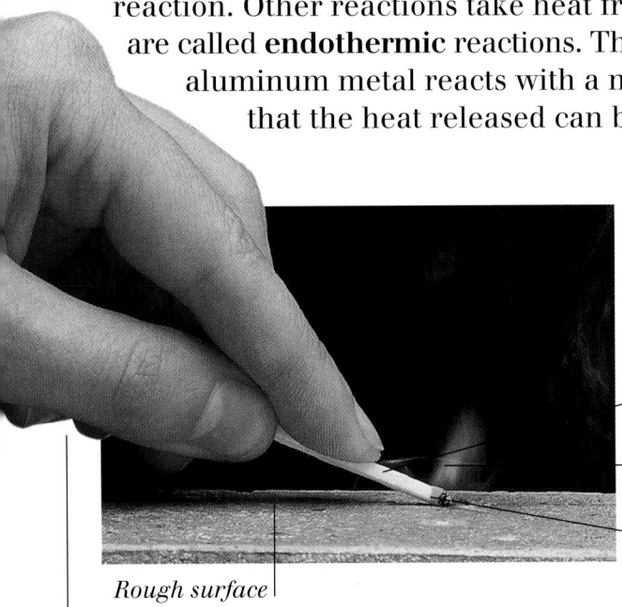

EXOTHERMIC AND ENDOTHERMIC REACTIONS

EXOTHERMIC REACTION, $CaCl_2 \rightarrow Ca^{2+} + 2Cl^-$
Compounds contain a certain amount of energy. If the energy of the **products** of a reaction is less than that of the **reactants**, then heat will be released to the surroundings. The reaction is described as exothermic. When calcium chloride dissolves in water, an exothermic reaction takes place.

ENDOTHERMIC REACTION, $NH_4NO_3 \rightarrow NH_4^+ + NO_3^-$
If the energy of the products of a reaction is more than that of the reactants, then heat will be taken from the surroundings. The reaction is described as endothermic. An endothermic reaction occurs when ammonium nitrate is dissolved in water.

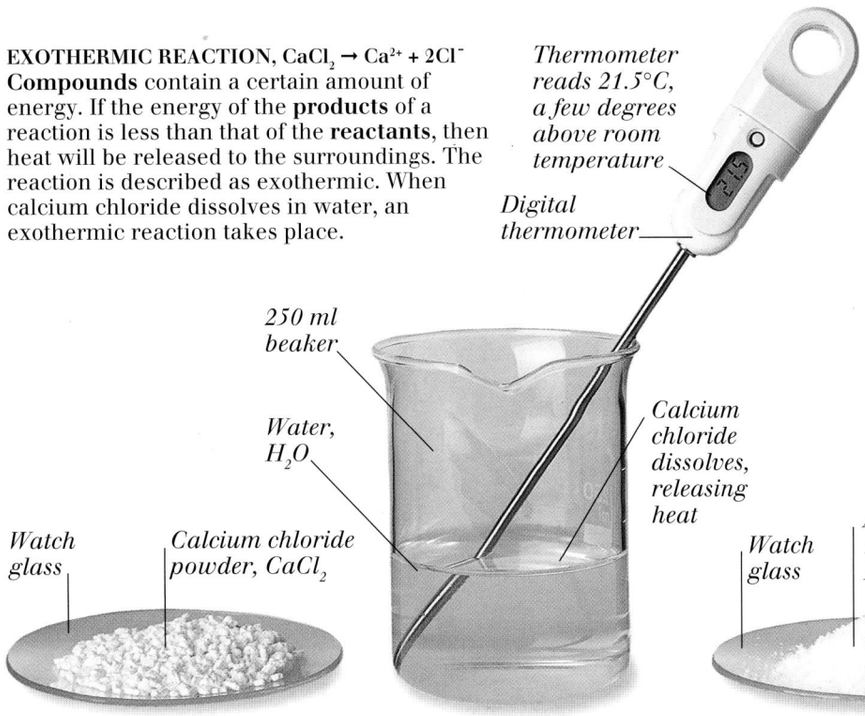

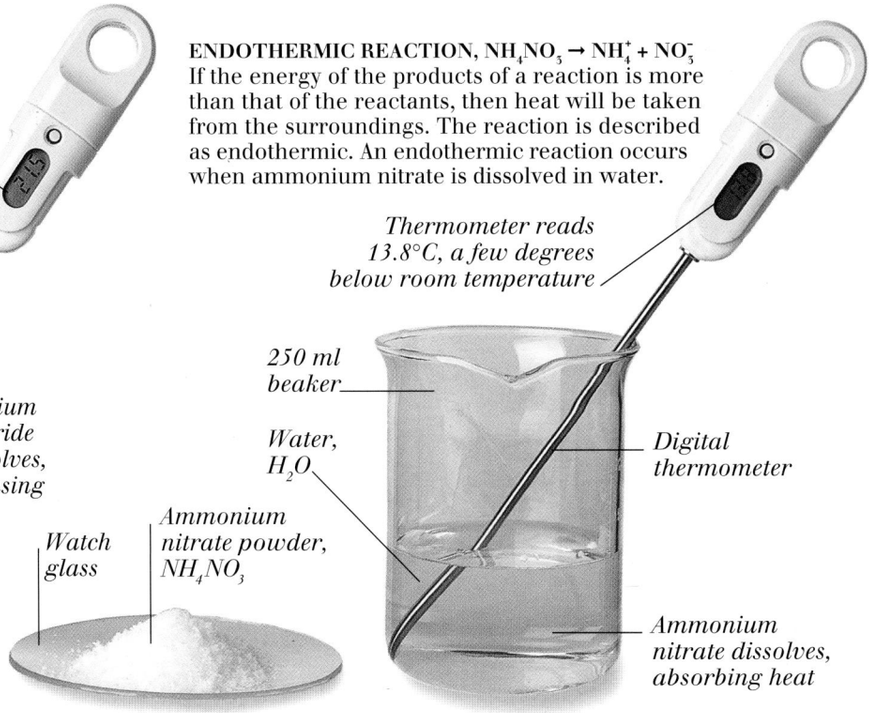

THERMITE REACTION

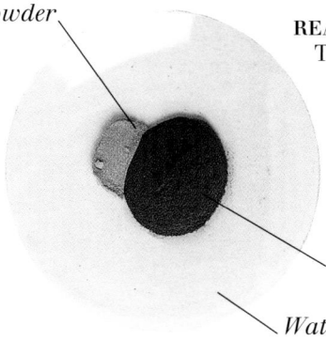

REACTANTS
The thermite reaction can take place between aluminum and many different metal oxides. Here, the reactants are aluminum and iron(III) oxide.

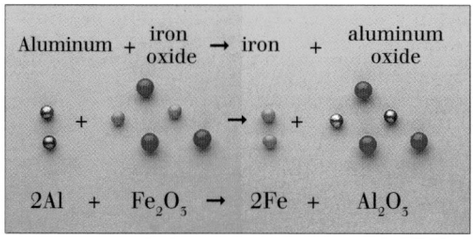

MOLECULAR MODEL OF REACTION

Thick smoke consists of small particles of reaction products

THERMITE WELDING

The tremendous amount of heat released by the thermite reaction is put to good use in welding railroad tracks. Iron oxide is used, yielding molten iron as one of the reaction products. The molten iron helps to make the weld.

THE REACTION
When aluminum reacts with iron(III) oxide, aluminum(III) oxide and iron are produced. Aluminum is a very **reactive** metal (see pp. 32–33), and has a greater affinity for oxygen than iron does. The reaction products have much less energy than the reactants, so the reaction of aluminum with iron(III) oxide is exothermic.

Burning magnesium strip provides the activation energy for the reaction

A large amount of heat is released

Metal tray

Products of the reaction are aluminum oxide and metallic iron

Flames

Shower of sparks

Water in chemistry

EACH MOLECULE OF WATER consists of two **atoms** of hydrogen bound to an oxygen atom. Water reacts physically and chemically with a wide range of **elements** and **compounds**. Many gases dissolve in water – in particular, ammonia dissolves very readily, as demonstrated by the fountain experiment. Some compounds, called **dehydrating agents**, have such a strong affinity for water that they can remove it from other substances. Concentrated sulfuric acid is so powerful a dehydrating agent that it can remove hydrogen and oxygen from certain compounds, making water where there was none before. Water is often held in **crystals** of other substances, and is then called **water of crystallization**. A compound can lose its water of crystallization during strong heating, and is then said to be **anhydrous**. Adding water to anhydrous crystals can restore the water of crystallization. Some compounds, described as **efflorescent**, have crystals that lose their water of crystallization to the air. Conversely, **hygroscopic** compounds have crystals that absorb water from the air. Desiccators often employ such compounds to dry other substances.

WATER OF CRYSTALLIZATION
Crystals containing water of crystallization are said to be hydrated. Heating a hydrated crystal causes it to lose water.

COPPER(II) SULFATE SOLUTION
Gently heating a **solution** of blue copper(II) sulfate evaporates the water, leaving behind blue crystals of hydrated copper(II) sulfate.

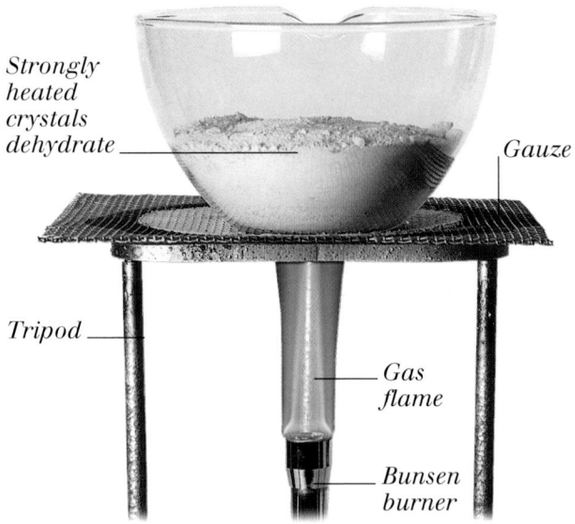

ANHYDROUS COPPER(II) SULFATE
Strongly heating the hydrated crystals drives off the water of crystallization, leaving a white powder of anhydrous copper(II) sulfate.

SULFURIC ACID AS A DEHYDRATING AGENT
Substances known as dehydrating agents can either simply remove water from a **mixture**, or remove hydrogen and oxygen from a compound in the ratio 2:1, the ratio found in water. Concentrated sulfuric acid is a very powerful dehydrating agent (below).

CONCENTRATED SULFURIC ACID, H_2SO_4

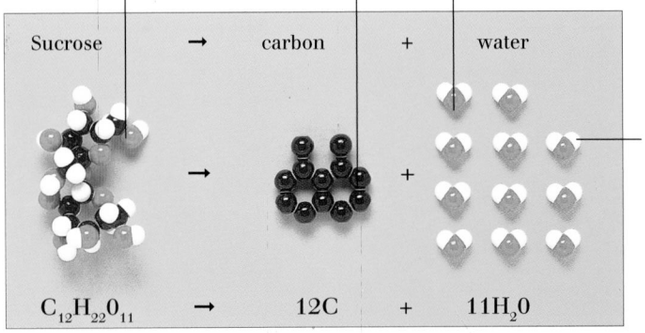

MOLECULAR MODEL OF REACTION

Each water molecule has two atoms of hydrogen and one of oxygen

DEHYDRATION OF SUCROSE
Concentrated sulfuric acid removes 22 hydrogen atoms and 11 oxygen atoms from each molecule of sucrose, leaving only black carbon behind. The reaction evolves heat, enough to boil the water produced and form steam.

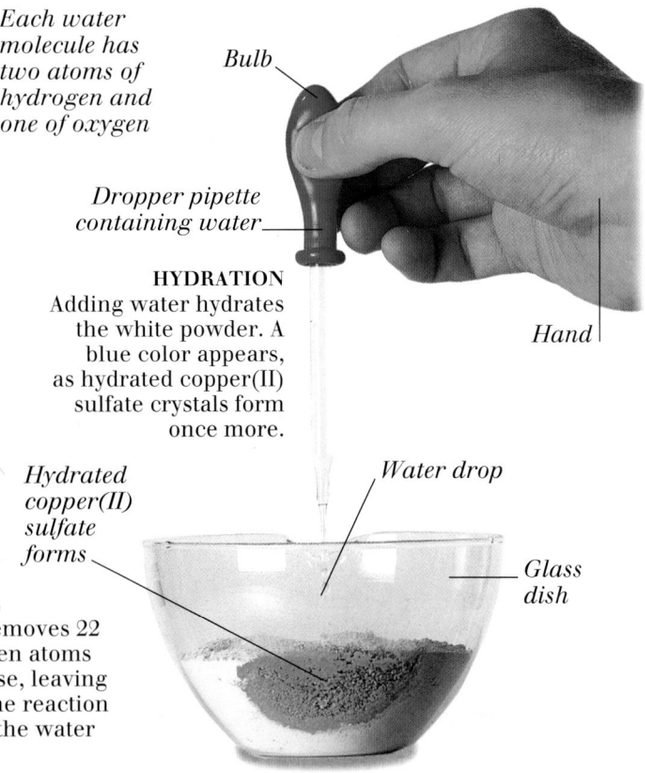

HYDRATION
Adding water hydrates the white powder. A blue color appears, as hydrated copper(II) sulfate crystals form once more.

AMMONIA FOUNTAIN

Water is a good solvent – even many gases dissolve in it. Ammonia dissolves very readily in water, forming an **alkaline solution** (see pp. 22–23). This fountain experiment employs red litmus solution, an **indicator** that turns blue in the presence of an alkali.

Indicator solution sprays up into the flask through the nozzle

Ammonia dissolves very readily

Partial vacuum forms

Nozzle

Round-bottomed flask

Clamp stand

Clamp

VACUUM IN A FLASK
Ammonia gas in a flask is in contact with a dish of water through a glass tube. As the ammonia dissolves in the water, it leaves behind a partial vacuum. Air pressure pushes water up the tube, and the nozzle at the end of the tube produces a fountain.

Litmus indicator turns blue, showing that water with ammonia dissolved is an alkaline solution

Rubber stopper

Glass tube

Valve

Red litmus shows that the water is slightly acidic

Air pressure on water pushes it up the tube

Glass dish

Water with indicator solution

EFFLORESCENCE AND HYGROSCOPY

In these two processes, compounds lose or gain water of crystallization. Efflorescent compounds lose their water of crystallization to the air. Hygroscopic compounds gain water from the air.

SODIUM CARBONATE DECAHYDRATE
The white crystals of sodium carbonate decahydrate (washing soda) shown here are efflorescent. Two sodium ions and a carbonate ion are combined with ten molecules of water of crystallization to form sodium carbonate decahydrate, $Na_2CO_3.10H_2O$.

SODIUM CARBONATE AFTER EXPOSURE TO AIR
When left in the air, the sodium carbonate decahydrate crystals give up most of the water of crystallization associated with them. The resulting white powder, called a monohydrate, is visible here on the surface of the crystals.

DESICCATOR

Some substances need to be kept free of moisture. A desiccator is a device that removes moisture. It is usually a glass container with a desiccant, or drying agent, inside.

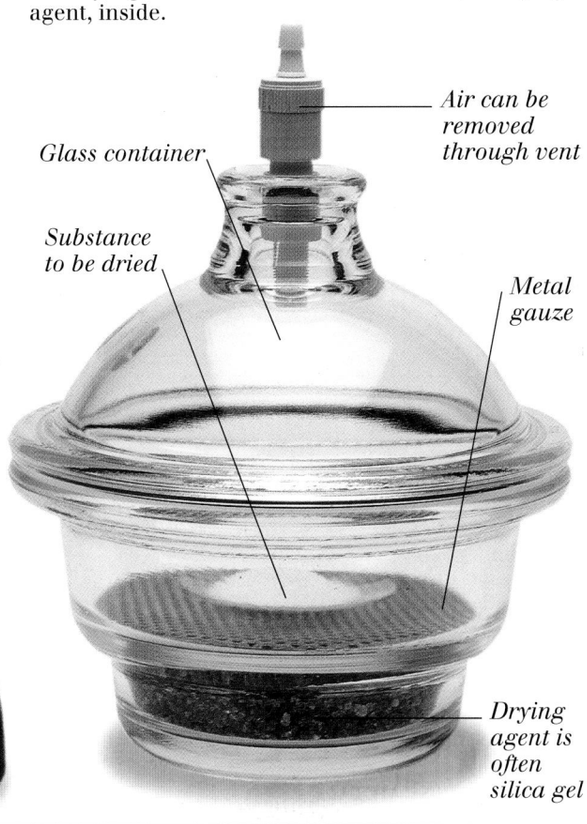

The activity series

ALL METAL ATOMS LOSE ELECTRONS fairly easily and become positive **ions**, or **cations**. The ease with which a metal loses **electrons** is a measure of its **reactivity**. Metals in groups 1 and 2 of the periodic table (see pp. 36–39), which have one and two outer electrons respectively, are usually the most reactive. Aluminum in group 3 is a reactive metal, but less so than calcium in group 2. Metals can be arranged in order of decreasing reactivity in a series known as the activity series. In this series, zinc is placed above copper, and copper above silver. Zinc metal is more reactive than copper and can displace copper ions from a **solution**. Similarly, copper displaces silver from solution. Electrons from the more reactive metal transfer to the less reactive metal ions in solution, resulting in the **deposition** of the less reactive metal. Because electron transfer occurs in these reactions, they are classified as **redox reactions**. The reactivity of a metal may be characterized in many ways – for example, by its reactions with **acids**. The different reactivities of metals have a practical application in the prevention of corrosion in underwater pipes.

TABLE OF METAL REACTIVITY

Metal	Air or oxygen on metal	Water on metal	Acids on metal	Metals on salts of other metals
K	Burn in air or oxygen	React with cold water (with decreasing ease)	Displace hydrogen from acids that are not oxidizing agents (with decreasing ease)	Displace a metal lower in the series from a solution of one of its salts
Na				
Ca				
Mg				
Al		React with steam when heated		
Zn				
Fe				
Sn	Converted into the oxide by heating in air	No reaction with water or steam		
Pb				
Cu			React only with oxidizing acids	
Hg				
Ag	Unaffected by air or oxygen			
Au			No reaction with acids	
Pt				

ALUMINUM METAL

REMOVING THE OXIDE LAYER
Metallic aluminum, which is used to make kitchen foil and saucepans, seems unreactive. Actually, aluminum is quite high in the activity series. When pure aluminum is exposed to the air, a thin layer of unreactive aluminum oxide rapidly forms on the surfaces, preventing further reaction.

DISPLACEMENT OF COPPER(II) IONS BY ZINC METAL
A **displacement reaction** is one in which **atoms** or ions of one substance take the place of atoms or ions of another. Here, zinc loses electrons to copper ions and displaces copper from a blue solution of copper(II) sulfate. The **products** of this reaction are copper metal and colorless zinc(II) sulfate solution.

ZINC METAL

COPPER(II) SULFATE SOLUTION

ZINC(II) SULFATE SOLUTION AND METALLIC COPPER

CATHODIC PROTECTION

PROTECTION OF OIL RIGS
Many metals corrode when exposed to water and air. To prevent underwater or underground metal pipes from corroding, a more reactive metal may be placed in contact with the pipe. Being more reactive, this metal corrodes in preference to the pipe. This technique, called cathodic protection, is commonly used in oil rigs.

REACTIONS OF METALS WITH DILUTE ACIDS

Acid solutions contain hydrogen ions, H^+, in the form of **hydronium ions**, H_3O^+ (see pp. 22–23). Reactive metals in an acid solution donate electrons to hydrogen ions, producing hydrogen gas. Metal atoms become positive ions and dissolve. The more reactive the metal, the faster the reaction proceeds. Some metals are so unreactive that they will only react with hot concentrated acid, and some will not react with acids at all.

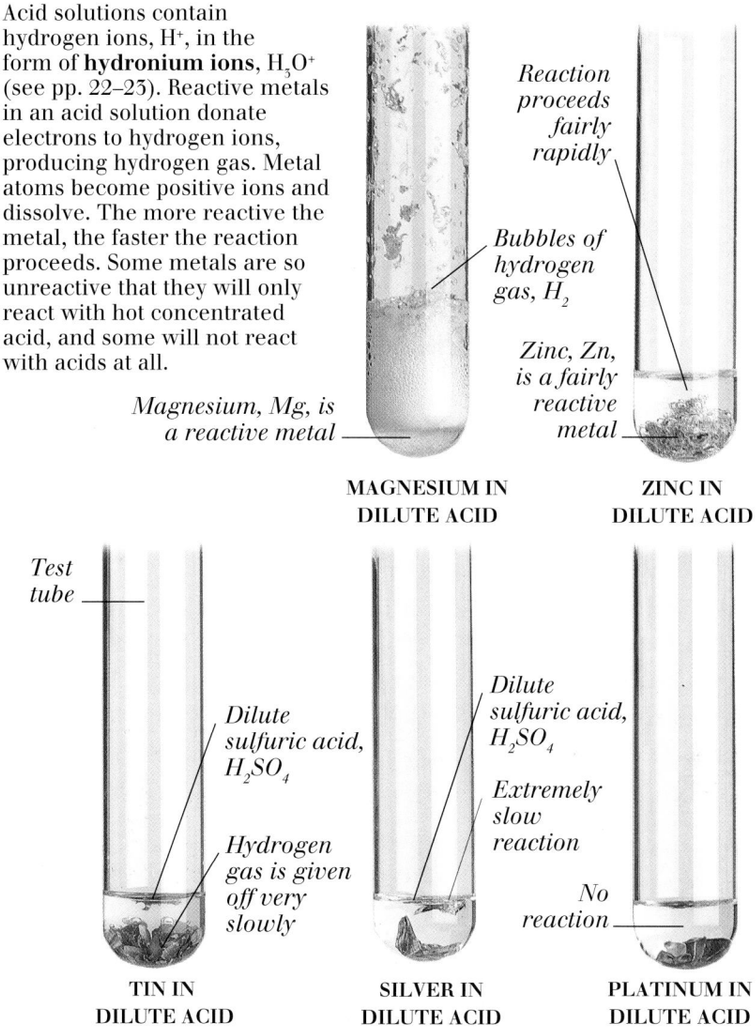

DISPLACEMENT OF SILVER(I) IONS BY COPPER METAL

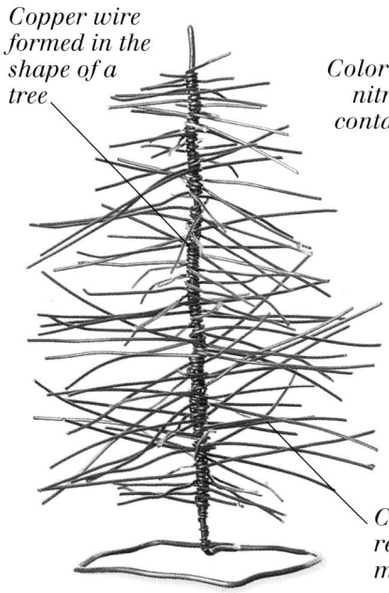

COPPER WIRE "TREE"
Here wire made from copper is formed into the shape of a tree. This shape has a large surface area, upon which the reaction can occur.

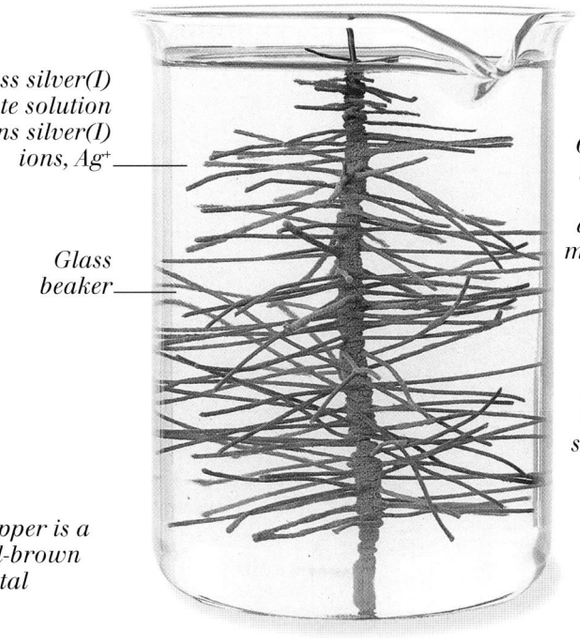

COPPER TREE IN SILVER NITRATE SOLUTION
When the copper wire is submerged in a solution of silver(I) nitrate, the copper metal loses electrons to the silver(I) ions.

DEPOSITION OF SILVER CRYSTALS
The silver ions are displaced to form silver metal, which coats the copper tree. A blue solution of copper(II) nitrate forms.

Electrochemistry

ELECTRICITY PLAYS A PART in all **chemical reactions**, because all **atoms** consist of **electrically charged** particles (see pp. 10-11). A flow of charged particles is called a current, and is usually carried around a circuit by **electrons**, moved by an electromotive force, or voltage. In **solution**, the charge carriers are **ions**, which are also moved by a voltage. A solution containing ions that conducts current is called an **electrolyte**. There are two basic types of electrochemical systems or cells. In an electrolytic cell, two conductors called **electrodes** are dipped in an electrolyte, and connected via an external circuit to a battery or other source of voltage. Such a cell can **decompose** the electrolyte in a process called **electrolysis**. Electrolytic cells are also used in the electroplating of metals. In a voltaic cell, electrodes of two different metals are dipped in an electrolyte. The electrodes produce a voltage that can drive a current between them. Voltaic cells are the basis of common batteries. In both types of cells, the **anode** is the electrode at which **oxidation** occurs, and the **cathode** the one where **reduction** occurs. The cathode is the positive terminal of voltaic cells, but negative in electrolytic cells.

ALKALINE DRY CELL (VOLTAIC)

Electrochemistry is put to use in this **alkaline** dry cell. Powdered zinc metal forms one electrode, while manganese(IV) oxide forms the other. This cell produces electricity at 1.5 volts. Batteries producing 3, 4.5, 6, or 9 volts are made by connecting a series of these cells.

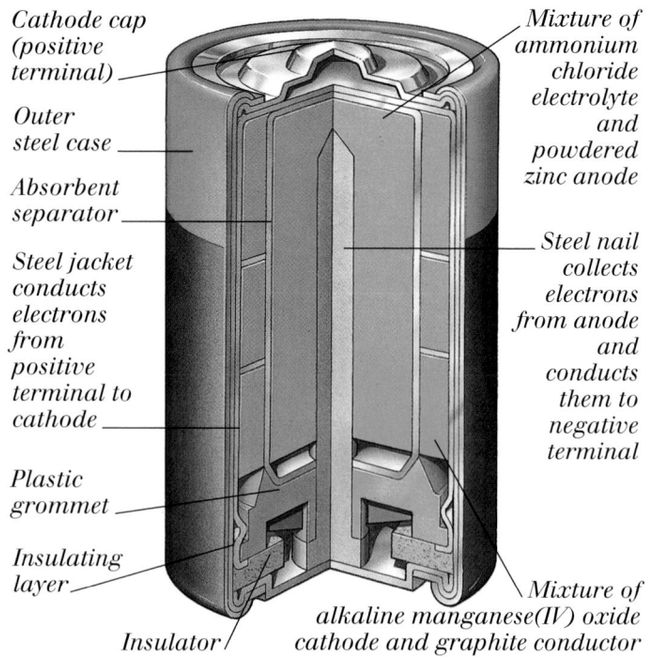

ELECTROLYSIS

ELECTROLYTIC DECOMPOSITION OF WATER
Passing an electric current through water decomposes it, producing the gases hydrogen and oxygen. A small amount of an **ionic compound** is dissolved in the water to make an electrolyte, into which two electrodes are dipped. The battery removes electrons, e^-, from one electrode, the anode, and pushes them toward the cathode. This is an example of an electrolytic cell.

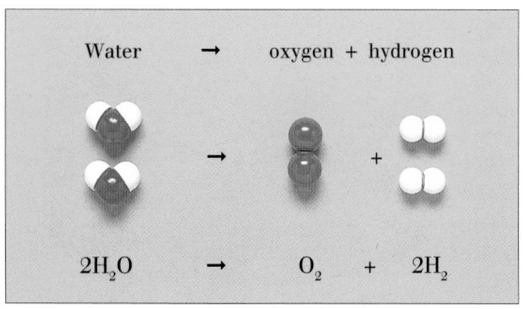

MOLECULAR VIEW OF OVERALL REACTION
Each **molecule** of water contains one oxygen and two hydrogen atoms. Both gases produced are **diatomic** – they have two atoms per molecule – so two hydrogen molecules are produced for each oxygen molecule.

Clamp
Upturned test tube collects oxygen gas
At the anode, the battery removes $4e^-$ from $4OH^-$, oxidizing them to $O_2 + 2H_2O$
Volume of hydrogen produced is twice that of oxygen
Graphite cathode
Upturned test tube
OH^- ions in electrolyte move toward anode
At the cathode, $4e^-$ are added to $4H_3O^+$, reducing water to $2H_2 + 4H_2O$
H_3O^+ ions in electrolyte move toward cathode
Graphite anode
Insulated electrical wire
Bubble of hydrogen gas
Bubble of oxygen gas
Alligator clip
Water with dissolved ions
Negative terminal
Positive terminal
500 ml beaker
4.5 volt battery

VOLTAIC CELL

PRODUCING A VOLTAGE
When two electrodes of different metals are dipped in an **acidic** solution so that they do not touch each other, an electric voltage is set up between them. This arrangement is called a voltaic cell. If the two electrodes are connected externally by a wire, the voltage causes an electric current to flow. In the voltaic cell below, zinc atoms are oxidized to zinc(II) ions at the anode. Electrons from this oxidation flow through the wire, illuminating the lightbulb, to the copper cathode, where hydrogen ions in solution are reduced to hydrogen gas.

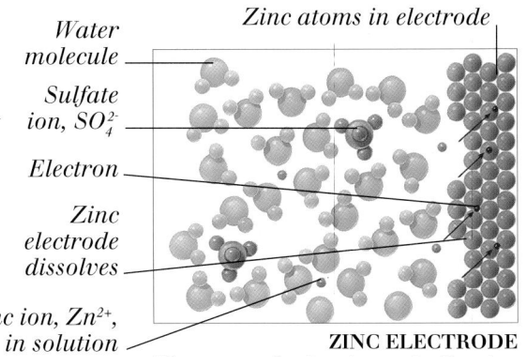

ZINC ELECTRODE
Zinc atoms in the electrode dissolve in the acid, losing electrons to form **cations.** Oxidation occurs, so this electrode is the anode.

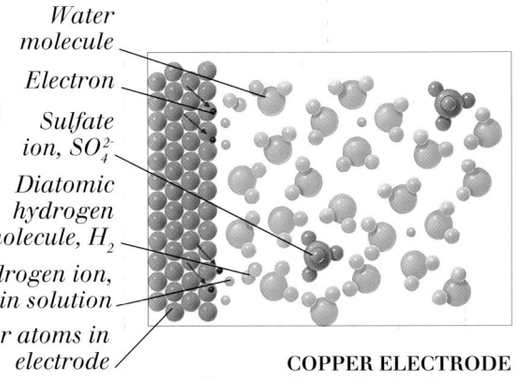

COPPER ELECTRODE
Here, at the cathode, electrons arrive from the zinc anode via the external circuit. They reduce hydrogen ions from the acid, forming hydrogen gas molecules.

ELECTROPLATING

COPPER PLATING A KEY
In electroplating, a thin layer of one metal is deposited onto the surface of another. The item to be plated is made the cathode in an electrolytic cell. The electrolyte is a solution containing ions of the other metal. Here, a brass key is plated with copper. The copper ions in solution are replenished from a copper anode.

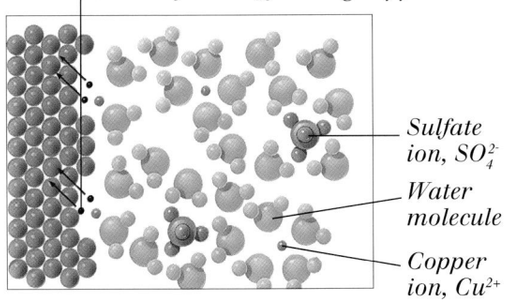

AT THE COPPER PIPE ANODE
The battery's positive terminal draws electrons from the anode, oxidizing the copper atoms to copper(II) cations. These ions dissolve and move toward the cathode.

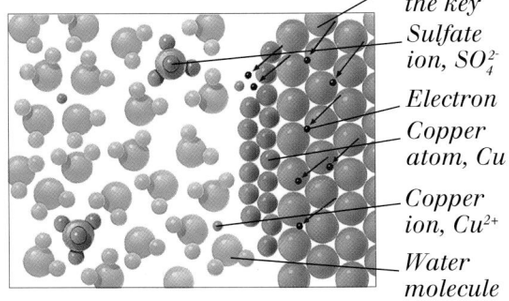

AT THE BRASS KEY CATHODE
Copper ions that have moved to the cathode are reduced to copper atoms by electrons from the battery. These atoms build up on the surface of the brass key cathode.

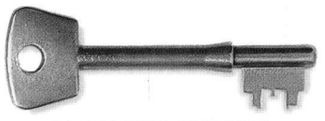

BRASS KEY (BEFORE)

COPPER-PLATED KEY (AFTER)

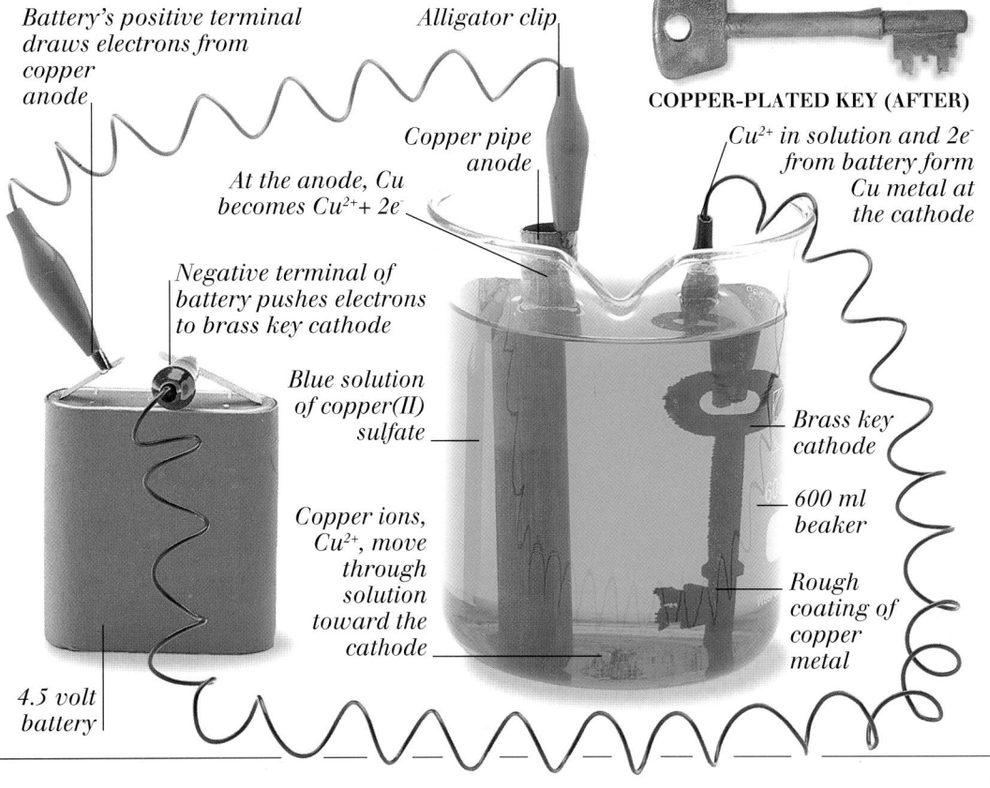

The alkali metals

THE ELEMENTS OF GROUP 1 of the periodic table (see pp. 12–13) are called the alkali metals. **Atoms** of these **elements** have one outer **electron**. This electron is easily lost, forming singly charged **cations** such as the lithium **ion**, Li^+. As with all cations, the lithium cation is smaller than the lithium atom. All of the elements in this group are highly **reactive** metals (see pp. 14–15). They react violently with **acids**, and even react with water to form **alkaline solutions** (see pp. 22–23) – hence their group name. The most important element in this group is sodium. Sodium forms many **compounds**, including sodium chloride, or common salt, and sodium hydrogencarbonate, which is used in baking powder. By far the most important compound of sodium in industrial use is sodium hydroxide. It is manufactured in large quantities, mainly by the **electrolysis** of brine (a solution of sodium chloride). Sodium hydroxide is a strong **base**, and it reacts with the fatty acids in fats and oils to produce soap, which is a **salt** (see pp. 24–25).

POSITION IN THE PERIODIC TABLE

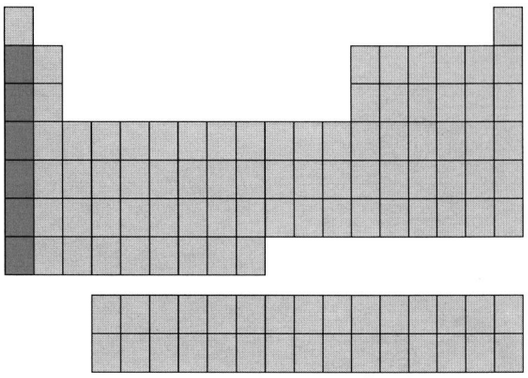

GROUP 1 ELEMENTS
The alkali metals form group 1 of the periodic table. They are (from top): lithium (Li), sodium (Na), potassium (K), rubidium (Rb), cesium (Cs), and francium (Fr).

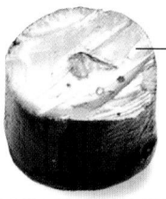

Potassium is a soft, silvery metal

POTASSIUM METAL

REACTION WITH WATER

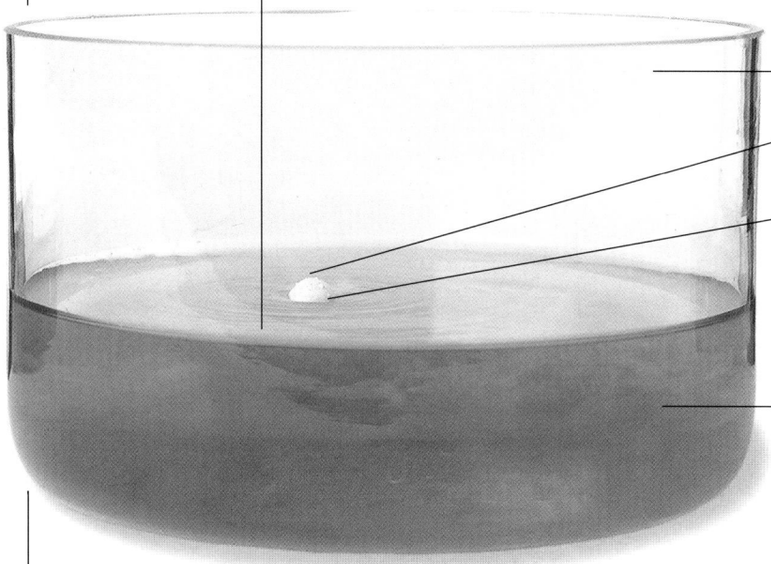

SODIUM IN INDICATOR SOLUTION
A piece of pure sodium metal reacts dangerously with water. Here, red litmus **indicator** is dissolved in the water. Explosive hydrogen gas is given off by the reaction, and the litmus turns blue with the resulting sodium hydroxide solution (above).

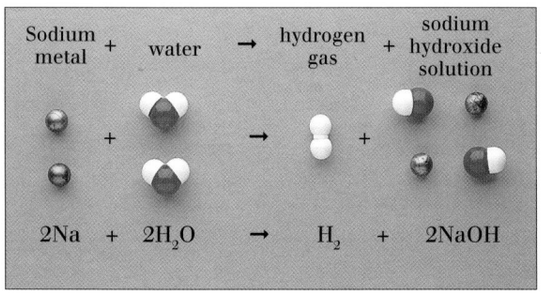

MOLECULAR VIEW
Sodium atoms lose electrons to form sodium cations, Na^+, which dissolve in water. Water **molecules** each gain an electron and split into a hydroxide **anion**, which dissolves, and a hydrogen atom. Two atoms of hydrogen combine to form hydrogen gas, H_2.

ATOMS AND CATIONS

Atoms of the alkali metals have one electron, which is easily lost, in their outer **electron shell**. The cation formed is much smaller than the atom. Atomic and ionic diameters are given below for the first four alkali metals, measured in picometers (1 picometer, pm, is 10^{-12} m). Electron configurations of the elements are also given.

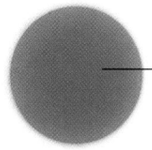

Atomic diameter 304 pm

LITHIUM ATOM, $1S^2\ 2S^1$

Ionic diameter 136 pm

LITHIUM ION, $1S^2$

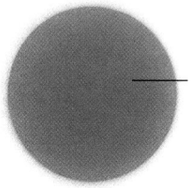

Atomic diameter 370 pm

SODIUM ATOM, $1S^2\ 2S^2\ 2P^6\ 3S^1$

Ionic diameter 194 pm

SODIUM ION, $1S^2\ 2S^2\ 2P^6$

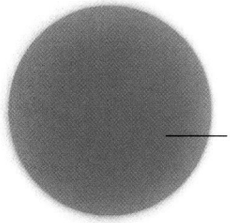

Atomic diameter 462 pm

POTASSIUM ATOM, $1S^2\ 2S^2\ 2P^6\ 3S^2\ 3P^6\ 4S^1$

Ionic diameter 266 pm

POTASSIUM ION, $1S^2\ 2S^2\ 2P^6\ 3S^2\ 3P^6$

Atomic diameter 492 pm

RUBIDIUM ATOM, $1S^2\ 2S^2\ 2P^6\ 3S^2\ 3P^6\ 3D^{10}\ 4S^2\ 4P^6\ 5S^1$

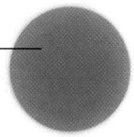

Ionic diameter 294 pm

RUBIDIUM ION, $1S^2\ 2S^2\ 2P^6\ 3S^2\ 3P^6\ 3D^{10}\ 4S^2\ 4P^6$

SODIUM HYDROGENCARBONATE

Sodium hydrogencarbonate, $NaHCO_3$ – also known as sodium bicarbonate – is a weak base that **decomposes** on heating or on reaction with an acid, releasing carbon dioxide gas (see pp. 22–23). This white powder is used as a rising agent in cooking, and is an important ingredient of soda bread.

MANUFACTURING OF SODIUM HYDROXIDE

Much of the sodium hydroxide, NaOH, manufactured is made by the mercury cathode process. This two-stage process begins with the electrolysis of brine, NaCl, to give chlorine gas and pure sodium. The sodium then reacts with water to give sodium hydroxide solution. Mercury is very toxic, and this process is banned in some countries.

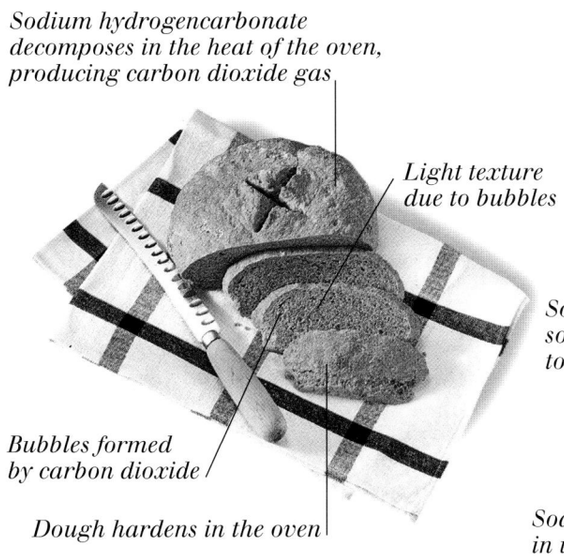

SODA BREAD

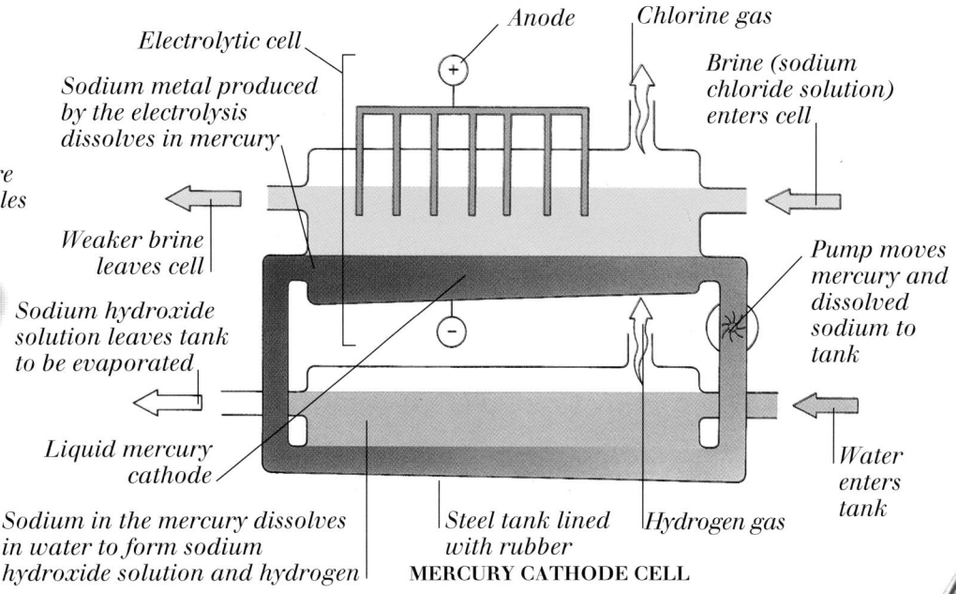

MERCURY CATHODE CELL

PRODUCTION OF SOAP

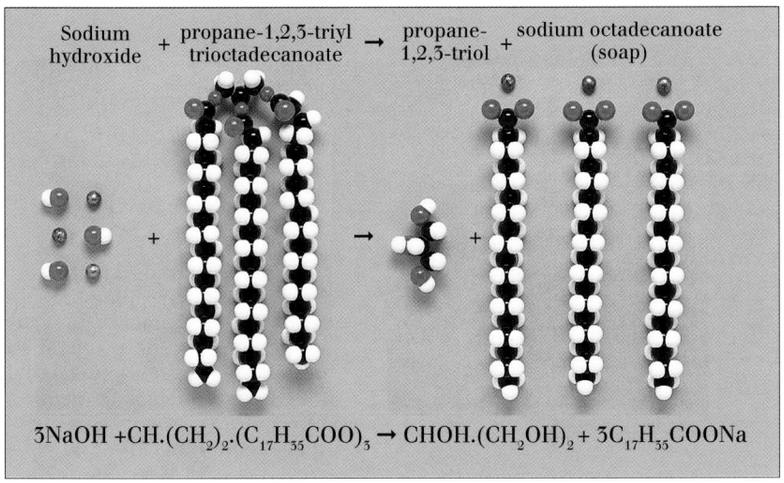

MOLECULAR VIEW
The oil molecule shown consists of three long-chain fatty acids linked by propane-1,2,3-triol (glycerol). Sodium hydroxide reacts with the fatty acids from the oil to produce glycerol and the salt sodium octadecanoate.

LABORATORY PREPARATION
When fatty acids – weak acids found in fats and oils – are heated with sodium hydroxide, a strong base, they react to produce a **mixture** of salts. The main product is the salt sodium octadecanoate, $C_{17}H_{35}COONa$ (a soap). Common salt (sodium chloride) helps to separate the soap from the mixture.

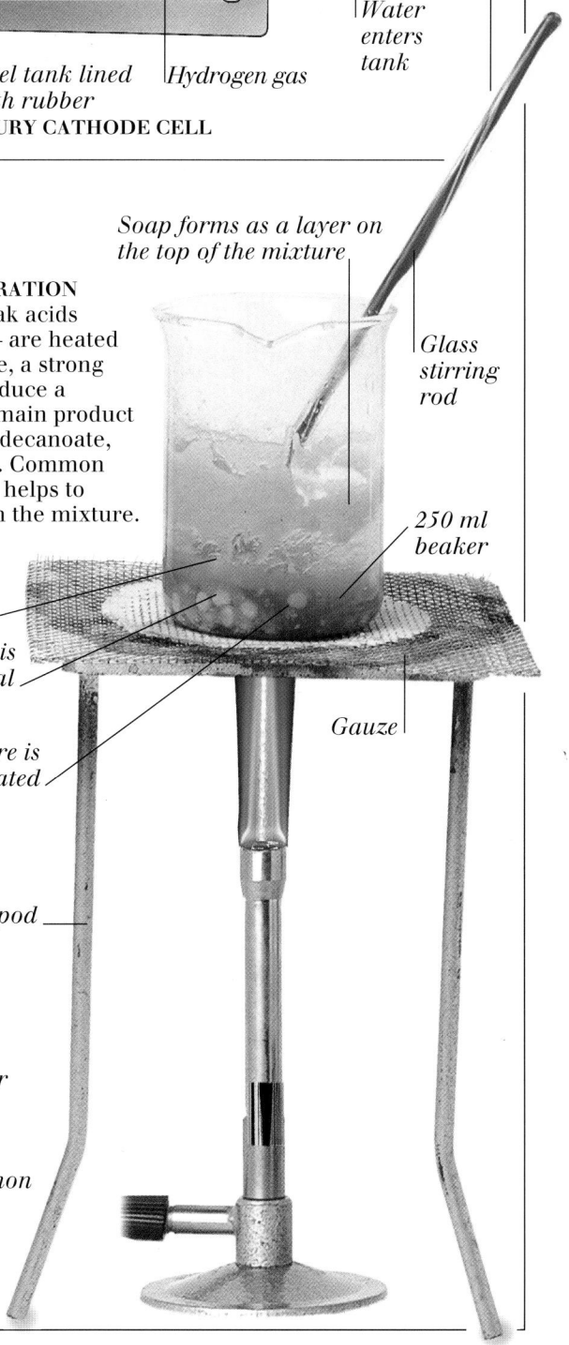

The alkaline earth metals

THE ELEMENTS OF THE SECOND GROUP of the periodic table (see pp. 12–13) are called the alkaline earth metals. These **elements** are **reactive**, because their **atoms** easily lose two outer **electrons** to form doubly charged **cations**, such as the calcium **ion**, Ca^{2+}. Hard water, which contains large numbers of dissolved ions, often contains calcium ions. It is formed when slightly **acidic** water flows over rocks containing calcium **salts** such as calcium carbonate. The dissolved calcium salts can come out of **solution** from hard water, forming the scale that blocks kettles and hot water pipes. It is difficult to create a lather with soap when using hard water. In fact, a simple way to measure the hardness of water is to **titrate** it with a soap solution. Calcium **compounds** are an important constituent of mortar, which is used as a cement in bricklaying. Magnesium, another group 2 element, is found in the pigment chlorophyll, which gives green plants their color. Alkaline earth metals are commonly used in the manufacture of fireworks, and barium is used in hospitals for the production of X-rays of the digestive system.

POSITION IN THE PERIODIC TABLE

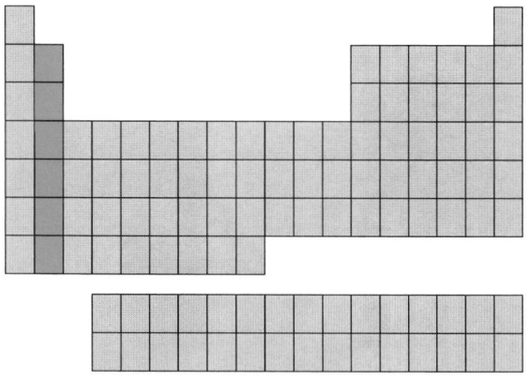

GROUP 2 ELEMENTS
The metals of group 2 of the periodic table are (from top): beryllium (Be), magnesium (Mg), calcium (Ca), strontium (Sr), barium (Ba), and radium (Ra).

MAGNESIUM IN CHLOROPHYLL

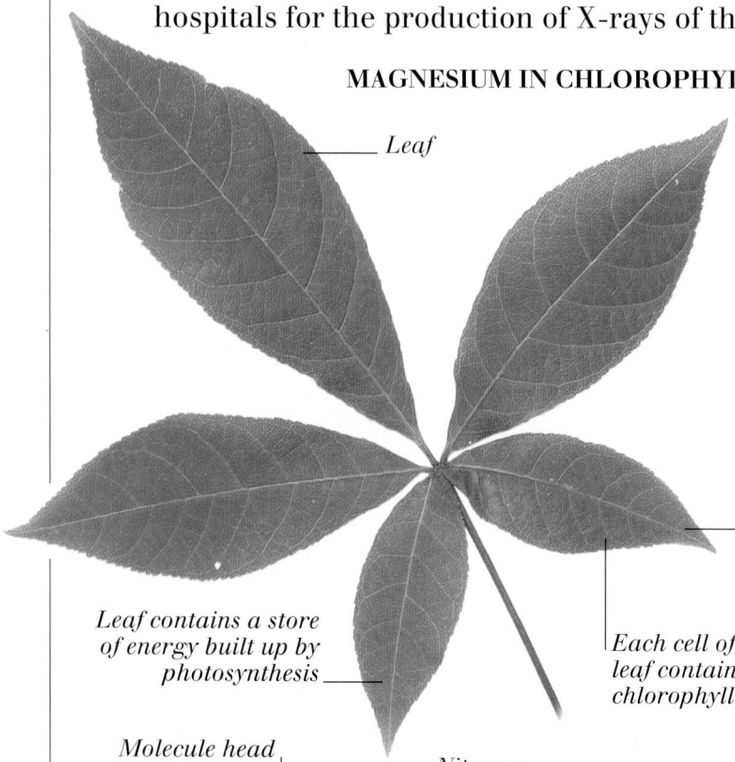

CHLOROPHYLL IN GREEN PLANTS
Green plants contain large amounts of a vital compound called chlorophyll. It absorbs **energy** from sunlight in a process called **photosynthesis**. The energy is used to make sugars (see pp. 52–53) from carbon dioxide and water.

Green color is caused by magnesium in chlorophyll pigment

HARDNESS OF WATER

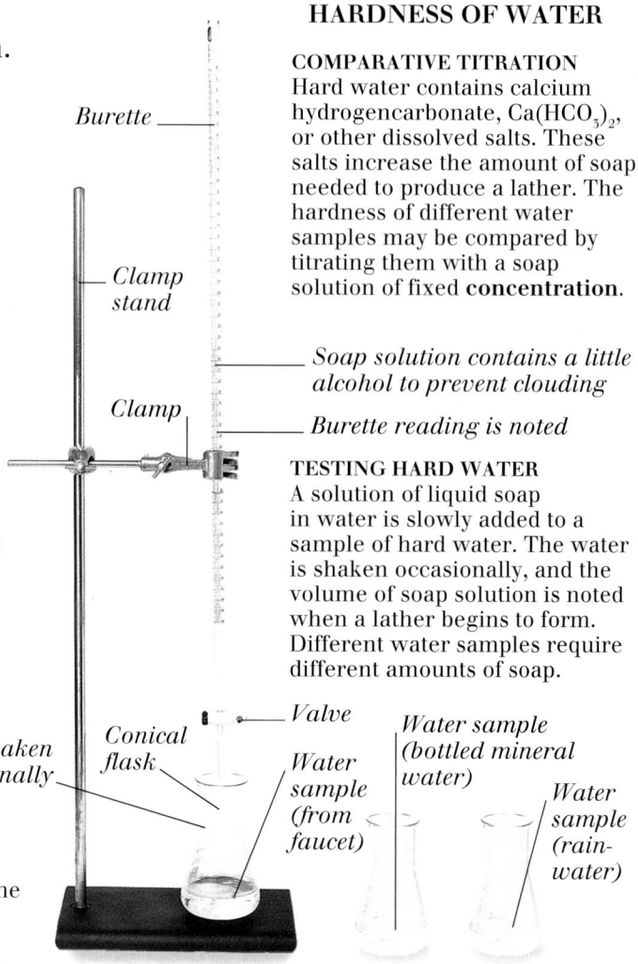

COMPARATIVE TITRATION
Hard water contains calcium hydrogencarbonate, $Ca(HCO_3)_2$, or other dissolved salts. These salts increase the amount of soap needed to produce a lather. The hardness of different water samples may be compared by titrating them with a soap solution of fixed **concentration**.

TESTING HARD WATER
A solution of liquid soap in water is slowly added to a sample of hard water. The water is shaken occasionally, and the volume of soap solution is noted when a lather begins to form. Different water samples require different amounts of soap.

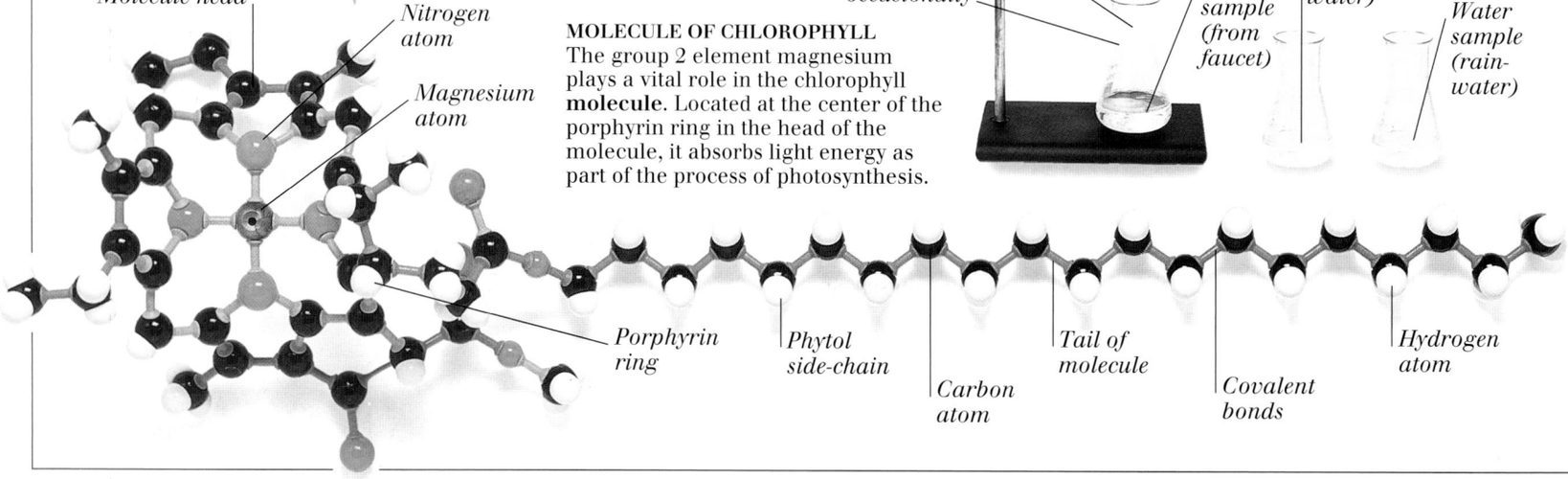

MOLECULE OF CHLOROPHYLL
The group 2 element magnesium plays a vital role in the chlorophyll **molecule**. Located at the center of the porphyrin ring in the head of the molecule, it absorbs light energy as part of the process of photosynthesis.

ALKALINE EARTH METALS IN FIREWORKS

CHARACTERISTIC COLORS
Group 2 elements produce bright colors when heated in a flame (see pp. 54–55). For this reason, compounds of the elements are used in fireworks. As gunpowder in the fireworks burns, electrons in the group 2 atoms absorb heat energy and radiate it out as light of characteristic colors.

BARIUM MEAL

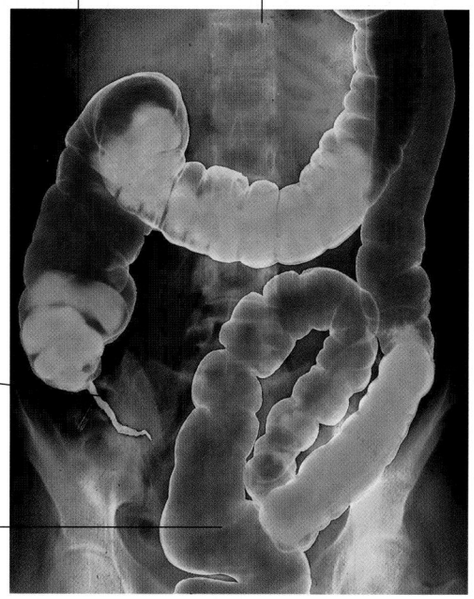

X-RAY PHOTOGRAPH OF DIGESTIVE SYSTEM
To obtain an X-ray of the digestive system, a "meal" of barium sulfate, $BaSO_4$, is administered to the patient. X-rays pass through human tissue, but are stopped by atoms of barium.

CALCIUM COMPOUNDS IN MORTAR

PRODUCTION OF MORTAR
Bricklayers' mortar is calcium hydroxide – also known as slaked lime, $Ca(OH)_2$ – dissolved in water, and mixed with sand for bulk. As the mixture dries, the slaked lime **crystallizes** out of solution, and slowly reacts with carbon dioxide in the air to form hard calcium carbonate (see below).

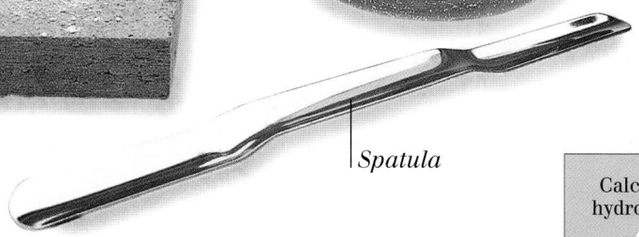

The ingredients are mixed thoroughly

MOLECULAR VIEW
Calcium ions, Ca^{2+}, and hydroxide ions, OH^-, form when slaked lime dissolves in water. Carbon dioxide, CO_2, combines with the ions as water leaves the mixture. This reaction is also the basis of a test for carbon dioxide (see pp. 54–55).

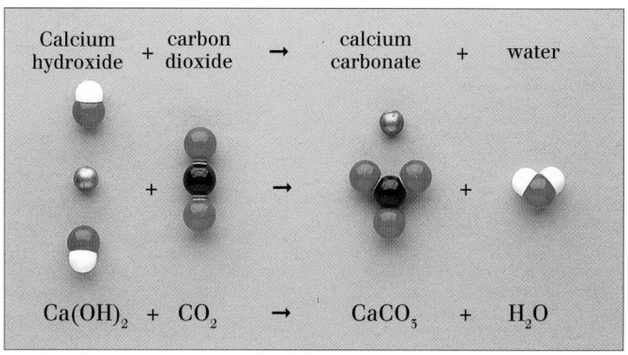

Transition metals

THE TRANSITION METALS MAKE UP MOST of the periodic table (see pp. 12–13). Some of the **elements** are very familiar – for example, gold and silver are used in jewelry, copper is used in electrical wiring and water pipes, and tungsten forms the filaments of incandescent light bulbs. **Transition metals** share many properties – for example, they all have more than one **oxidation number**. In **compounds**, chromium commonly has oxidation numbers of +2, +3, or +6. Like most transition metals, it forms colored **ions** in **solution**, such as the chromate(VI) and the dichromate(VI) ions. Copper also exhibits typical transition metal behavior – it forms brightly colored compounds and **complex ions**. Perhaps the most important of the transition metals is iron. It is the most widely used of all metals, and is usually **alloyed** with precise amounts of carbon and other elements to form steel. Around 770 million tons of steel are produced per year worldwide, most of it by the basic oxygen process. Chromium is used in stainless steel alloys, and as a shiny protective plating on other metals.

POSITION IN THE PERIODIC TABLE

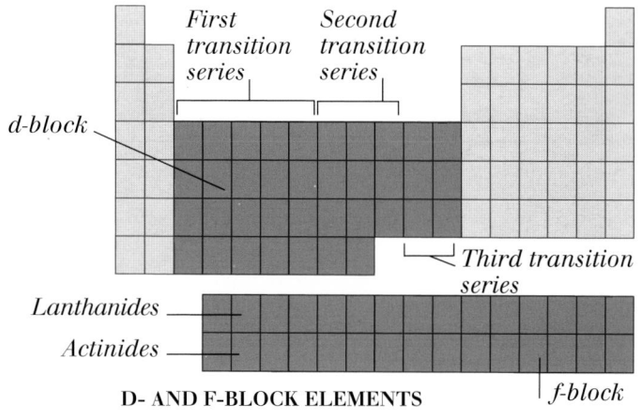

D- AND F-BLOCK ELEMENTS
Most of the transition metals lie in the d-block of the periodic table. The lanthanides and actinides, in the f-block, are also transition metals.

THREE D-BLOCK TRANSITION METALS

Gold is very unreactive

GOLD

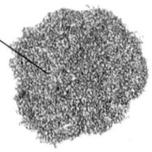
Silver compounds are used in photographic film

SILVER

Platinum is often used as a catalyst

PLATINUM

THREE TRANSITION METAL COMPOUNDS

Like many chromium compounds, chromium(III) oxide, Cr_2O_3, is used as a pigment

CHROMIUM(III) OXIDE

Chromium(VI) oxide, CrO_3, is highly poisonous

CHROMIUM(VI) OXIDE

This form of lead(II) oxide is called litharge

LEAD(II) OXIDE

COPPER – A TRANSITION METAL

COMPOUNDS OF COPPER
Like most of the transition metals, copper forms brightly colored compounds. All of the compounds shown here are of copper(II), and they all contain the ion Cu^{2+}.

Copper(II) oxide, CuO, is used as a catalyst in a number of reactions

COPPER(II) OXIDE

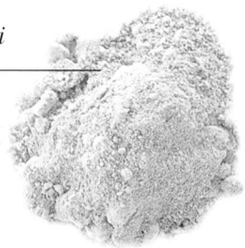
Copper(II) hydroxide can be prepared by adding a strong alkali to copper(II) salts

COPPER(II) HYDROXIDE

COPPER(II) NITRATE
Copper(II) nitrate is hygroscopic, which means that it absorbs water from the air

Copper(II) carbonate contains the carbonate radical, CO_3^{2-}

COPPER(II) CARBONATE

This blue-green sample of copper(II) chloride contains water of crystallization

COPPER(II) CHLORIDE

Red-brown copper turnings

Copper was one of the first metals to be used by humans

COPPER METAL

MANUFACTURE OF STEEL

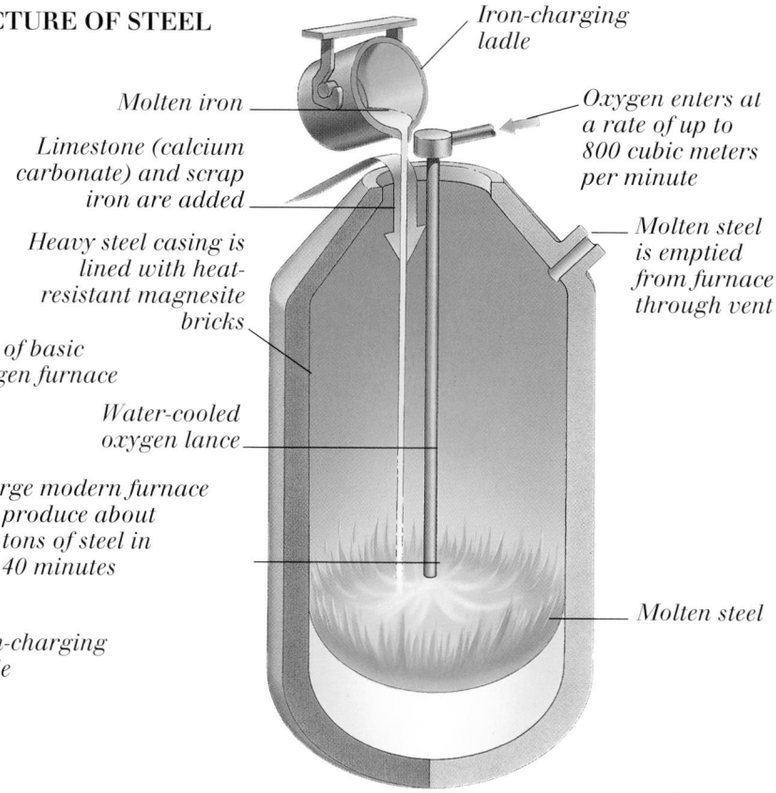

THE BASIC OXYGEN PROCESS
More than half the world's steel is produced by the basic oxygen process. This photograph shows a basic oxygen furnace (right) being charged, or filled, with molten iron.

BASIC OXYGEN FURNACE
Iron from a blast furnace is tipped into the basic oxygen furnace. Oxygen is pumped in to purify the iron by combining with carbon impurities. When the "blow" of oxygen is complete, the furnace is tilted to empty the steel.

CHROMATE IONS IN A REVERSIBLE REACTION

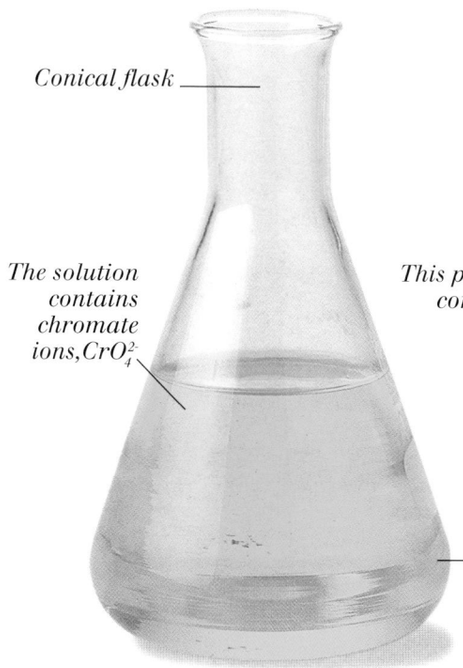

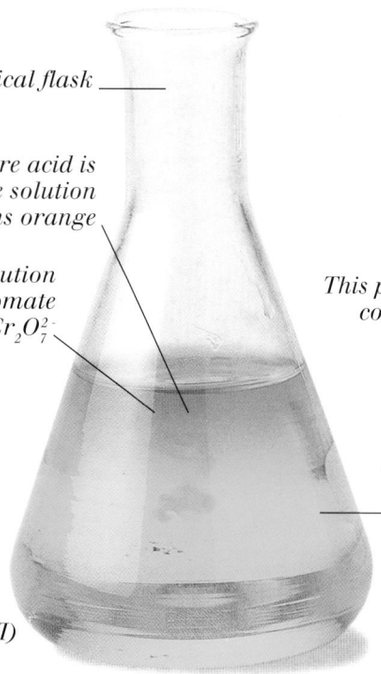

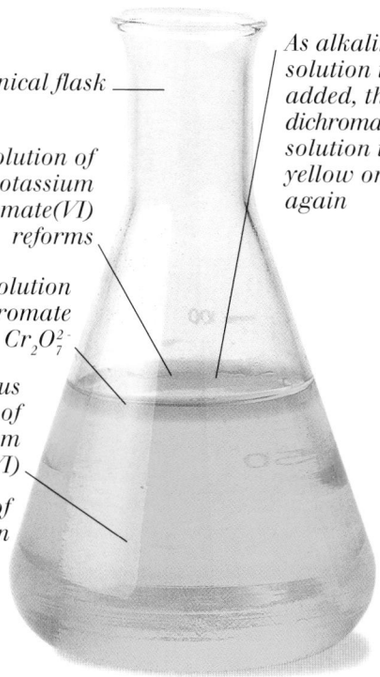

POTASSIUM CHROMATE SOLUTION
When dissolved in water, the compound potassium chromate(VI), K_2CrO_4, has a bright yellow color. Chromium in the compound has an oxidation number of +6.

POTASSIUM DICHROMATE SOLUTION
Adding an **acid** to the solution moves the position of the **equilibrium**. Two chromate(VI) ions combine to produce the dichromate(VI) ion, $Cr_2O_7^{2-}$, and water.

THE REVERSE REACTION
The addition of more water or an **alkaline** solution will push the **reversible reaction** in the direction of the original **reactants**. A yellow solution of chromate(VI) ions forms once more.

Carbon, silicon, and tin

GROUP 14 OF THE periodic table (see pp. 14–15) contains the **elements** carbon, silicon, and tin. Carbon is a nonmetal that is the basis of **organic** chemistry (see pp. 50–53). It occurs in three distinct forms, or **allotropes**. In the most recently discovered of these, called the fullerenes, carbon **atoms** join together in a hollow spherical cage. The other, more familiar, allotropes of carbon are graphite and diamond. All of the elements in group 14 form sp **hybrid orbitals** (see p. 17). In particular, sp^3 hybrid orbitals give a tetrahedral structure to many of the **compounds** of these elements. Silicon is a semimetal that is used in electronic components. It is found naturally in many types of rock, including quartz, which consists of silicon(IV) oxide. Quartz is the main constituent of sand, which is used to make glass. Tin is a metallic element. It is not very useful in its pure form because it is soft and weak. However, combined with other metals, it forms useful **alloys**, such as solder and bronze.

POSITION IN THE PERIODIC TABLE

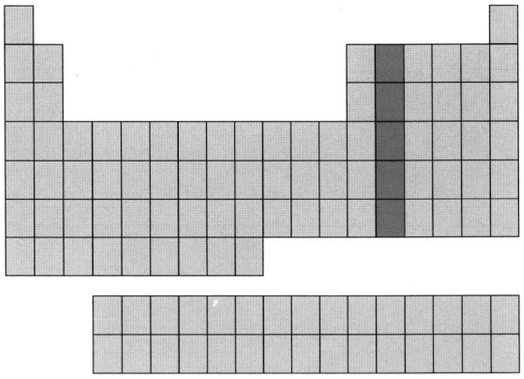

GROUP 14 ELEMENTS
Group 14 of the periodic table consists of (top to bottom): carbon(C), silicon (Si), germanium (Ge), tin (Sn), and lead (Pb).

THE ELEMENTS

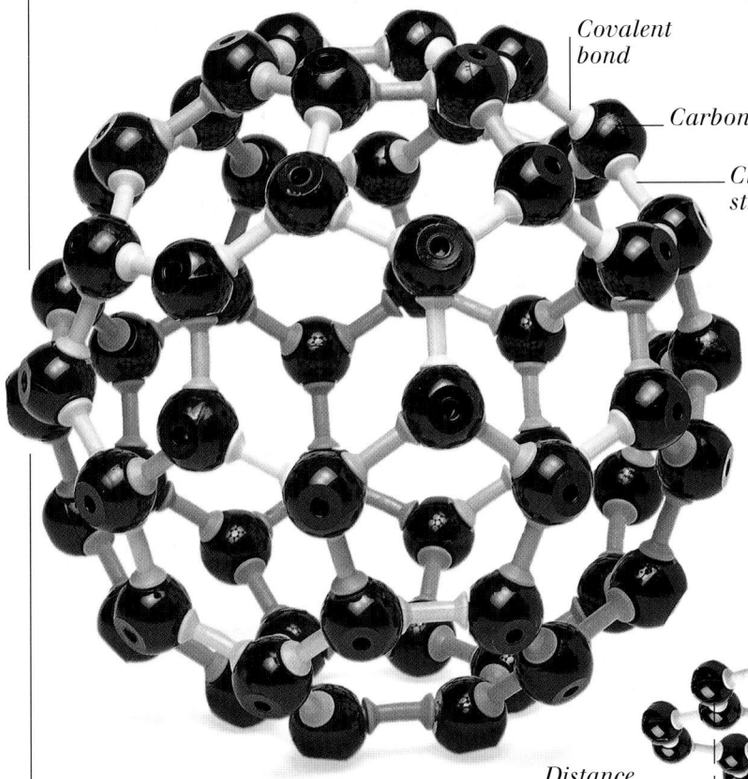

BUCKMINSTERFULLERENE, C_{60}
Carbon atoms form network structures called fullerenes. The best-known of these is buckminsterfullerene, which consists of 60 carbon atoms arranged as interlinked hexagons and pentagons. It occurs in nature in minute amounts, but can be made in the laboratory.

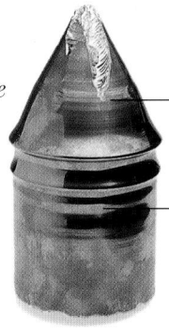

SILICON CRYSTAL
The element silicon can be made into large, pure **crystals**, which can be used to make thousands of silicon chips. These chips are the basis of microelectronic circuits.

ALLOTROPES OF CARBON
The main allotropes of carbon are graphite and diamond (below). In charcoal, carbon does not have a regular structure.

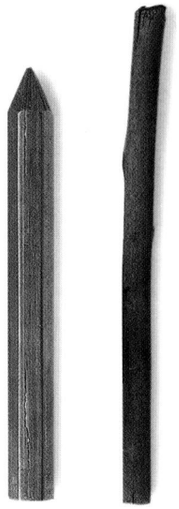

DIAMOND **GRAPHITE IN PENCIL "LEAD"** **CHARCOAL**

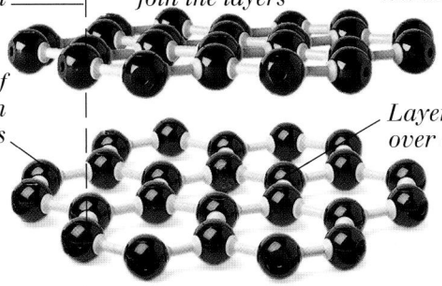

STRUCTURE OF GRAPHITE
Graphite is an allotrope of carbon which, combined with various clays, forms the "lead" of pencils. The carbon atoms in graphite form layers that are loosely bound together, and slip easily over each other.

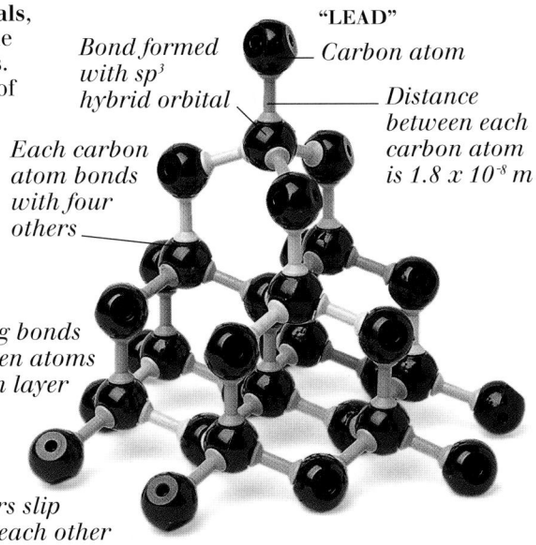

STRUCTURE OF DIAMOND
The carbon atoms in a diamond are bonded in a very strong structure. Each carbon atom is bound directly to four others, which sit at the corners of a tetrahedron.

SP^3 HYBRIDIZATION

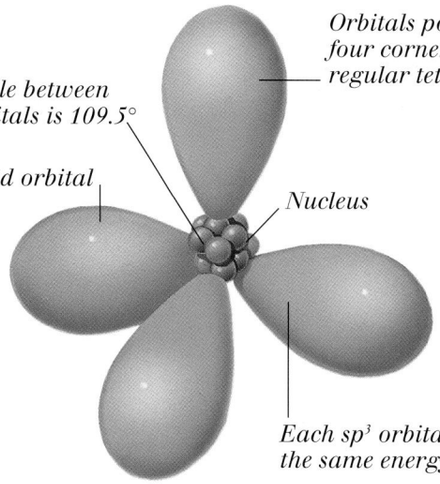

FORMATION OF SP^3 ORBITALS
The elements in group 14 of the periodic table have one s- and three p-orbitals in their outer **electron shells**. These combine to form four sp^3 hybrid orbitals in many of the compounds of the elements.

QUARTZ AND GLASS

QUARTZ
Quartz is the most abundant rock type on Earth. It consists mainly of the compound silicon(IV) oxide.

GLASS
Glass is made from molten sand, which consists mainly of quartz (above). Sodium and calcium **salts** are added to lower the melting point of the sand. The glass can be colored by adding impurities such as barium carbonate and iron(III) oxide.

BROWN GLASS BOTTLE

GREEN GLASS BOTTLE

Sodium carbonate lowers the melting point of sand, but makes the glass soluble in water

SODIUM CARBONATE

Calcium carbonate lowers the melting point of sand without making the glass soluble in water

CALCIUM CARBONATE

Sand consists of grains of quartz

SAND (MAINLY QUARTZ)

Barium carbonate gives glass a brown color

BARIUM CARBONATE

Iron(III) oxide gives glass a green color

IRON(III) OXIDE

ALLOYS OF TIN

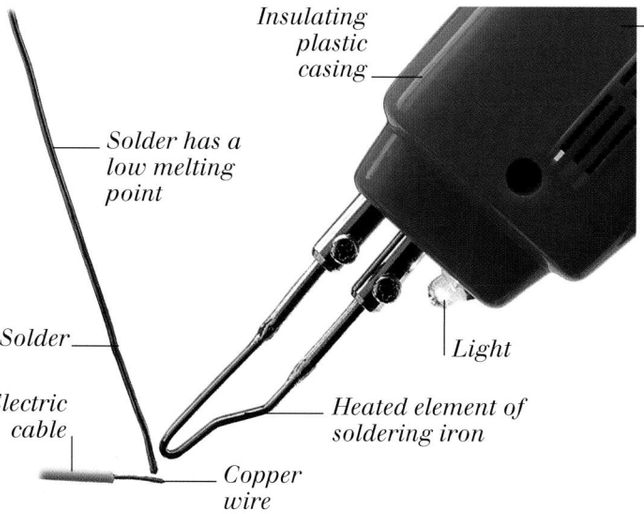

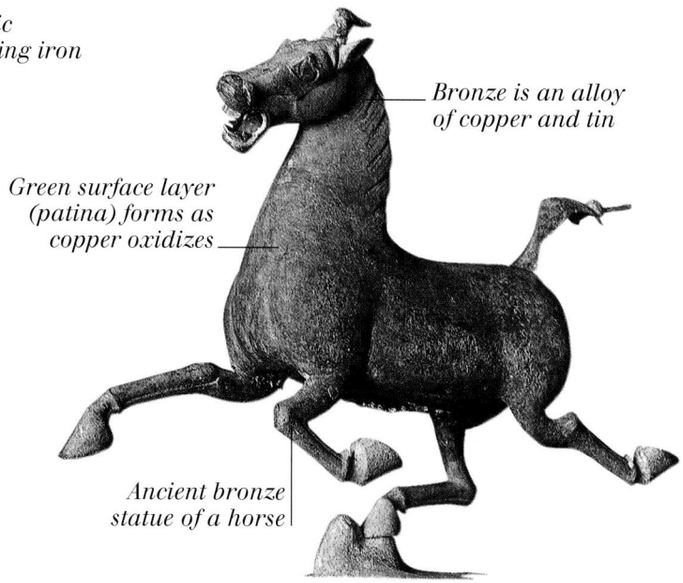

SOLDER
The most convenient way to connect wires and components permanently in electric circuits is to use solder. Solder is a soft alloy of tin and lead that has a low melting point (200–300°C).

BRONZE
First made about 5,000 years ago, bronze is an alloy of tin and copper (see pp. 40–41). It is easily cast when molten, but very hard-wearing when solidified.

Nitrogen and phosphorus

NITROGEN AND PHOSPHORUS are the two most important **elements** in group 15 of the periodic table (see pp. 12–13). Phosphorus, which is solid at room temperature, occurs in two forms, or **allotropes**, called white and red phosphorus. Nitrogen is a gas at room temperature, and makes up about 78% of air (see pp. 8–9). Fairly pure nitrogen can be prepared in the laboratory by removing oxygen, water vapor, and carbon dioxide from air. By far the most important **compound** of nitrogen is ammonia (see pp. 30–31), of which over 88 million tons are produced each year worldwide. Used in the manufacture of fertilizers, explosives, and nitric acid, ammonia is produced industrially by the Haber process, for which nitrogen and hydrogen are the raw materials. Ammonia forms a positive **ion** called the ammonium ion (NH_4^+) that occurs in **salts**, where it acts like a metal **cation** (see pp. 14–15). Ammonia can be prepared in the laboratory by heating an ammonium salt with an **alkali**, such as calcium hydroxide.

THE POSITION OF NITROGEN AND PHOSPHORUS IN THE PERIODIC TABLE

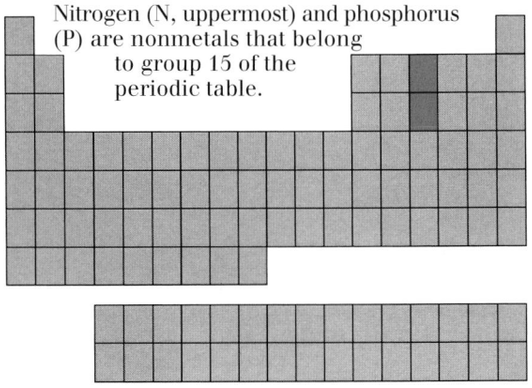

ALLOTROPES OF PHOSPHORUS

There are two common allotropes of phosphorus. White phosphorus reacts violently with air, so it is kept in water, in which it does not dissolve. It changes slowly to the noncrystalline red form, which is chemically less reactive.

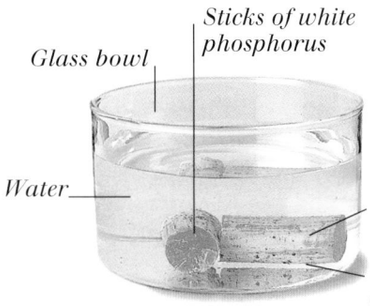

WHITE PHOSPHORUS

RED PHOSPHORUS

PREPARATION OF NITROGEN FROM AIR

Nitrogen is the most abundant gas in the air. Other gases that make up more than 1% of the air are oxygen (about 20%) and water vapor (0–4%). Air is passed through sodium hydroxide **solution**, which dissolves the small amounts of carbon dioxide present. It is then passed through concentrated sulfuric acid to remove water vapor, and, finally, over heated copper metal to remove oxygen. The result is almost pure nitrogen.

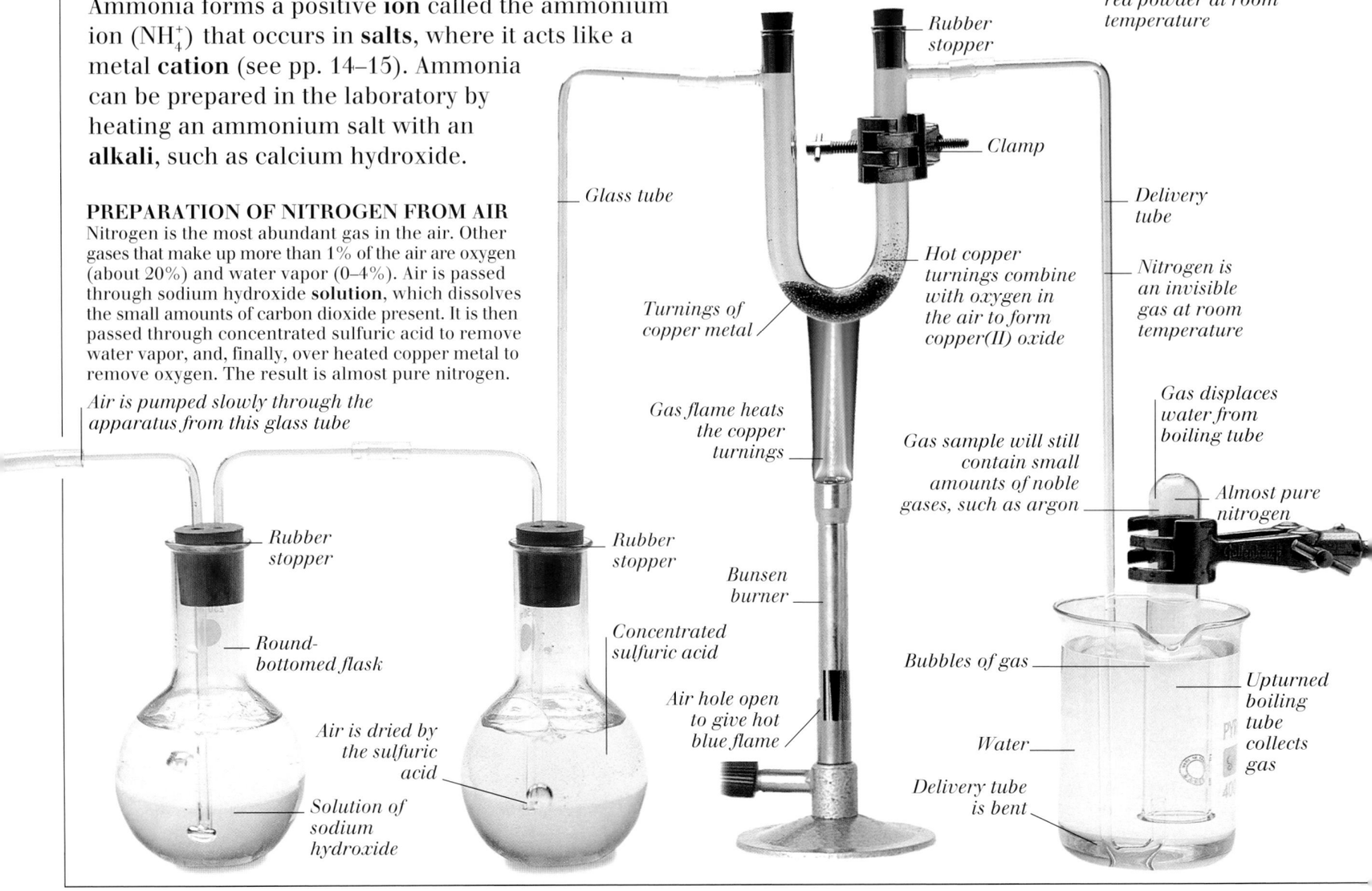

THE HABER PROCESS

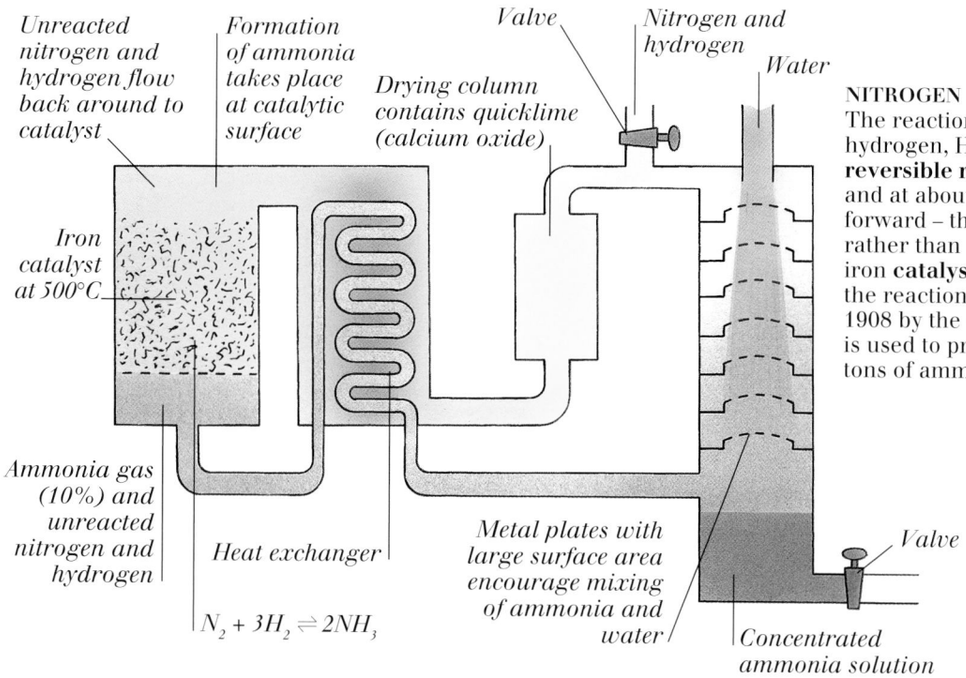

NITROGEN + HYDROGEN ⇌ AMMONIA
The reaction of nitrogen, N_2, and hydrogen, H_2, to form ammonia, NH_3, is a **reversible reaction**. Under high pressure and at about 450°C, the reaction proceeds forward – that is, it produces ammonia rather than nitrogen and hydrogen. An iron **catalyst** is used, which speeds up the reaction. This process, invented in 1908 by the German chemist Fritz Haber, is used to produce more than 88 million tons of ammonia annually.

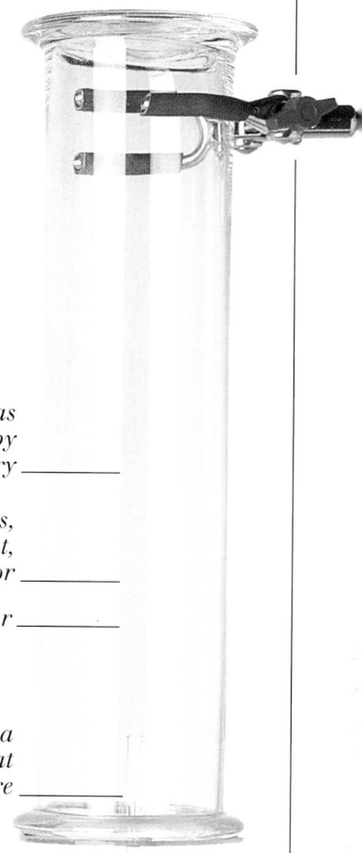

LABORATORY PREPARATION OF AMMONIA

In the laboratory, ammonia can be prepared by heating an ammonium salt with an alkali. Here, ammonium chloride, NH_4Cl, and calcium hydroxide, $Ca(OH)_2$, are heated in a flask. The ammonia produced is dried and collected in a gas jar.

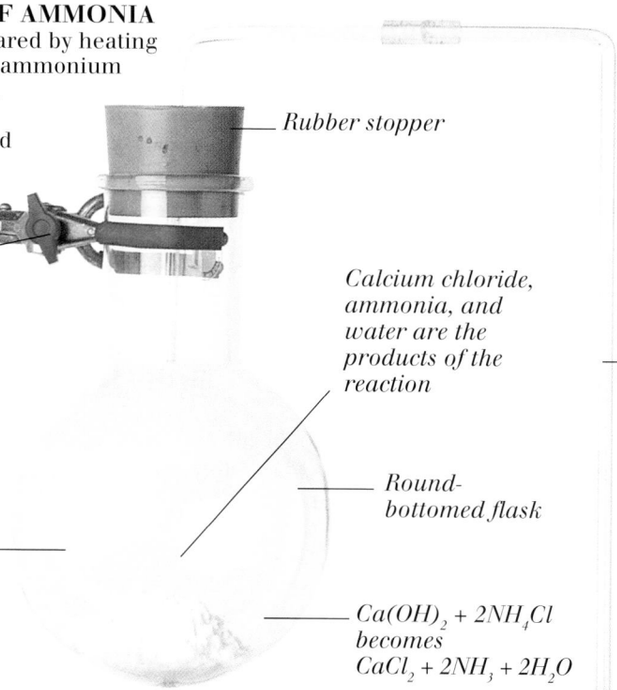

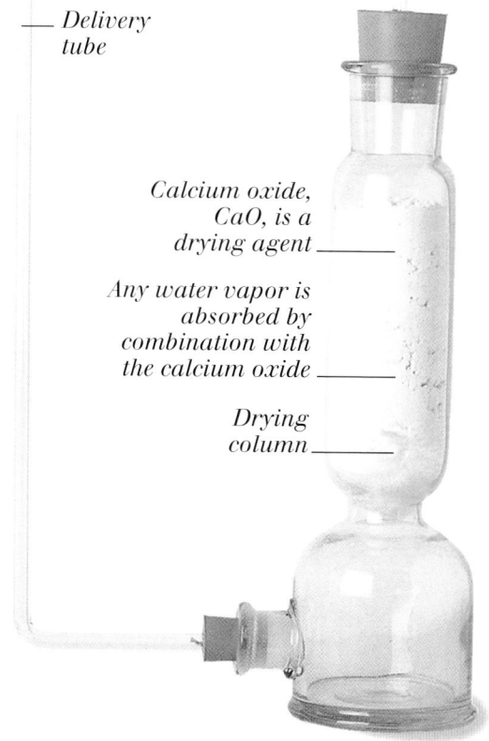

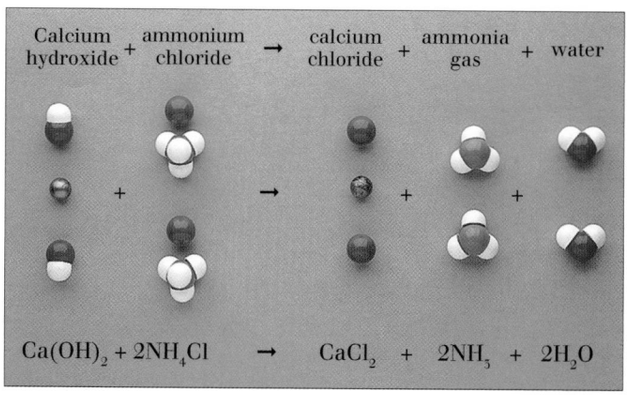

MOLECULAR VIEW OF REACTION

Oxygen and sulfur

THE TWO MOST IMPORTANT **elements** in group 16 of the periodic table are oxygen and sulfur. Oxygen, a gas at room temperature, is vital to life, and is one of the most abundant elements on Earth. It makes up 21% by volume of dry air (see pp. 8–9). In the laboratory, oxygen is easily prepared by the **decomposition** of hydrogen peroxide. Oxygen is involved in **burning** – it relights a glowing wooden splint, and this is one test for the gas. Sulfur occurs in several different structural forms, known as **allotropes**. The most stable allotrope at room temperature is rhombic sulfur, in which sulfur exists in the form of rings, each containing eight atoms. One important **compound** of sulfur is hydrogen sulfide. It has a pungent smell like that of rotten eggs, and can be prepared by reacting dilute **acids** with metal sulfides. Sodium thiosulfate is another important sulfur compound. It is used as a fixer in the development of photographic images.

POSITION IN THE PERIODIC TABLE

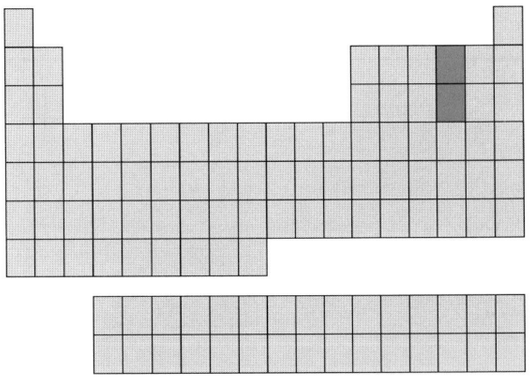

GROUP 16 ELEMENTS
Oxygen (top) and sulfur are in group 16 of the periodic table. They are both nonmetallic elements, which form a wide range of compounds.

TEST FOR OXYGEN

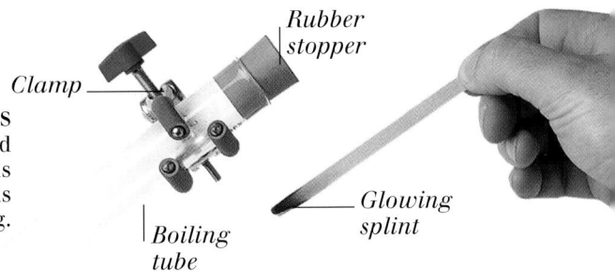

OXYGEN GAS
A tube full of oxygen gas, produced in the reaction on the left, is sealed. A previously lit splint is extinguished, but left glowing.

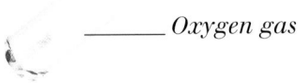

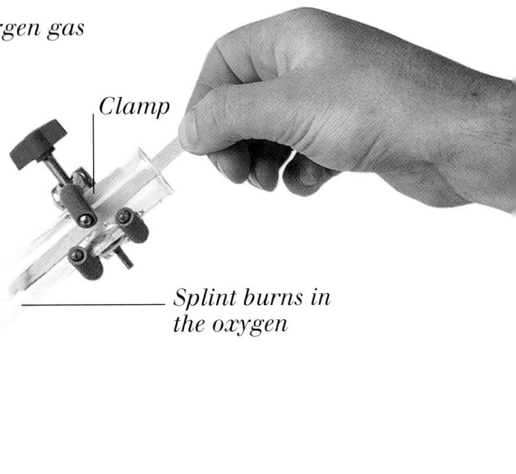

RELIT SPLINT
The glowing splint (above) relights in the oxygen. Burning, or combustion, is defined as a rapid combination of a substance with oxygen. It is a **redox reaction** (see pp. 20–21).

PREPARATION OF OXYGEN

Separating funnel
Hydrogen peroxide
Valve
Synthetic rubber connector
Rubber stopper
Glass delivery tube
Clamp
Round-bottomed flask
Water and oxygen are the products of the reaction
Mixture of manganese(IV) oxide and hydrogen peroxide
Oxygen gas fills the boiling tube
Clamp
Upturned boiling tube
Glass dish
Water

CATALYTIC DECOMPOSITION OF HYDROGEN PEROXIDE
The decomposition of hydrogen peroxide to oxygen and water normally occurs very slowly. The addition of a **catalyst** of manganese(IV) oxide to hydrogen peroxide speeds up the reaction.

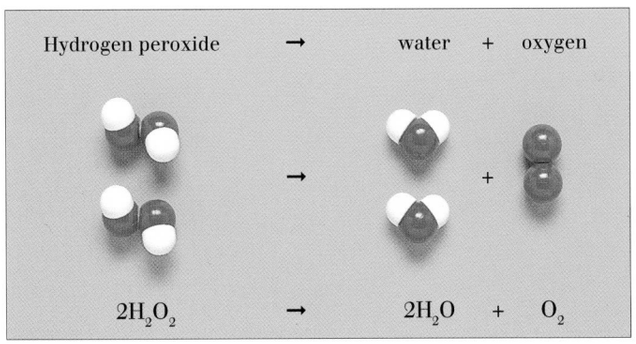

MOLECULAR VIEW
Hydrogen peroxide exists as **molecules**, each consisting of two hydrogen and two oxygen **atoms**. Every two molecules of hydrogen peroxide produce one molecule of oxygen. Water is the other **product**.

ALLOTROPES OF SULFUR

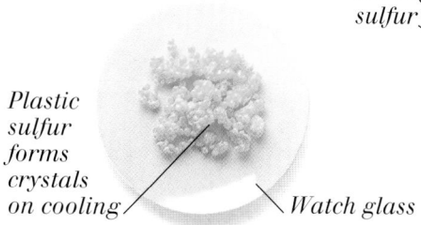

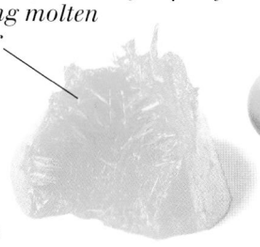

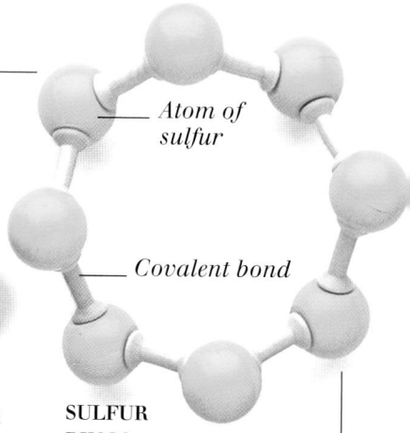

POWDERED SULFUR
In the laboratory, sulfur is usually supplied as a powder. Each grain of the powder is a crystal of rhombic sulfur (right).

RHOMBIC (α) SULFUR
The most stable allotrope of sulfur at room temperature is rhombic sulfur, also known as alpha (α) sulfur.

PLASTIC SULFUR
If molten sulfur is cooled by plunging it into cold water, yellow or brown plastic sulfur, which is noncrystalline, forms.

MONOCLINIC (β) SULFUR
Needlelike crystals of monoclinic (β, or beta) sulfur slowly revert to the rhombic form at temperatures below 95.5°C (203.9°F).

SULFUR RINGS
Monoclinic and rhombic sulfur both contain crown-shaped molecules of eight sulfur atoms.

LABORATORY PREPARATION OF HYDROGEN SULFIDE

The pungent gas hydrogen sulfide, H_2S, is normally prepared by the action of a dilute acid on metal sulfides. In this case, the reactants are hydrochloric acid, HCl, and iron(II) sulfide, FeS.

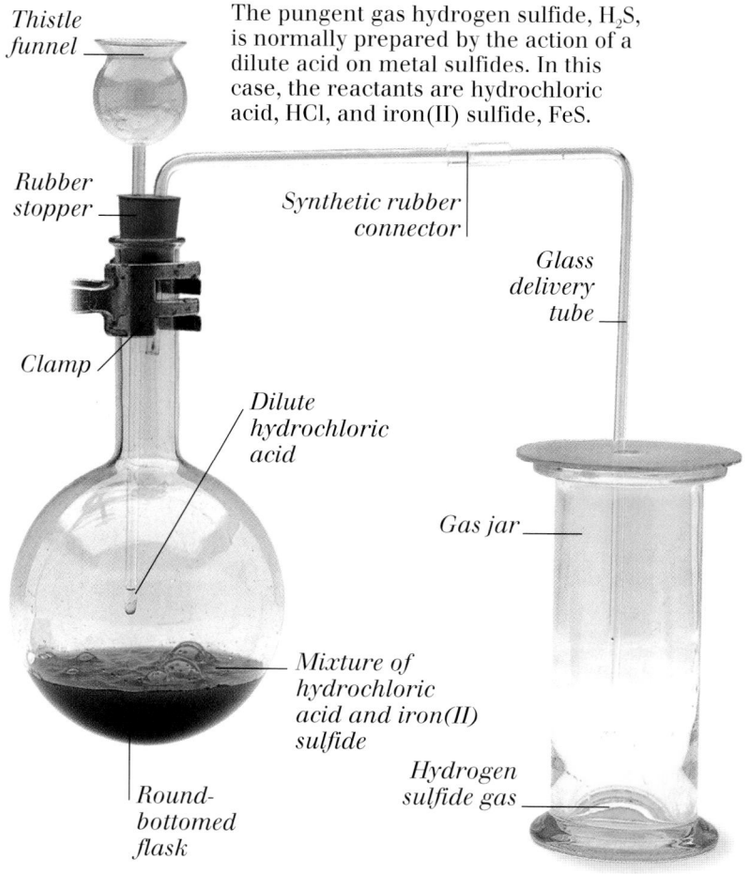

PREPARATION OF SODIUM THIOSULFATE

The compound sodium thiosulfate, $Na_2S_2O_3$, is normally combined with water of crystallization. It is used as photographers' fixer, "hypo." Sodium thiosulfate is prepared by heating a **suspension** of sulfur in a sodium sulfite, Na_2SO_3, **solution**.

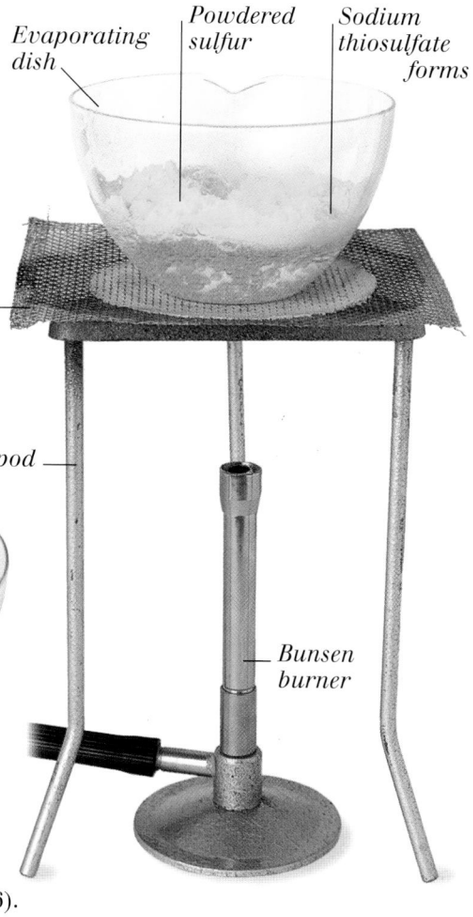

PRODUCT OF REACTION
Sodium thiosulfate (above) fixes photographic images by dissolving the silver halides, such as silver bromide, used in photographic film (see p. 26).

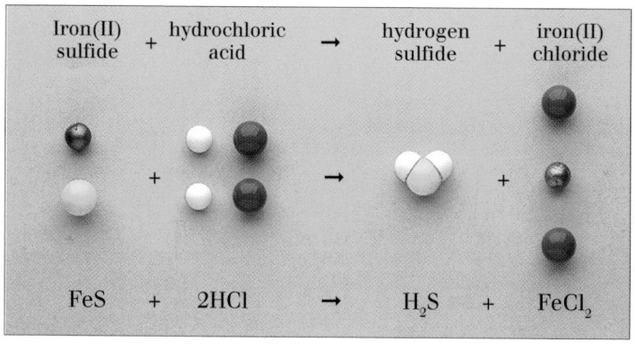

MOLECULAR VIEW
Hydrogen ions in hydrochloric acid combine with the sulfur from iron(II) sulfide. Hydrogen sulfide molecules have a similar shape to water molecules (see p. 6).

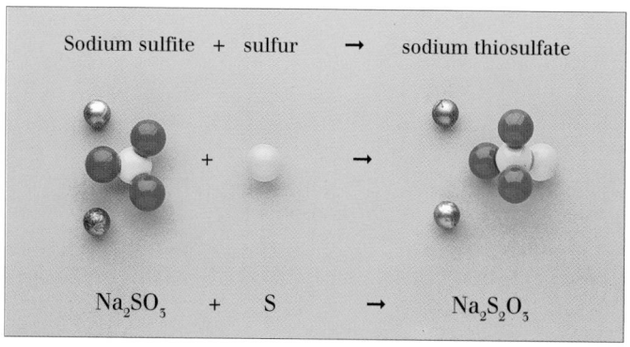

MOLECULAR VIEW
Sulfur in the sulfite ion has an **oxidation number** of +4. In the thiosulfate ion produced by the reaction above, sulfur(IV) has been **oxidized** to sulfur(VI), while elemental sulfur has been **reduced** to an oxidation state of -2.

The halogens

THE ELEMENTS OF GROUP 17 of the periodic table (see pp. 12–13) are called the halogens. **Atoms** of these **elements** are just one **electron** short of a full outer **electron shell**. Halogen atoms easily gain single electrons, forming singly charged halide **anions** such as the fluoride **ion**, F^-. This makes the elements in this group highly **reactive** – some halogens will even react with the **noble gases** under extreme conditions. Chlorine, the most important halogen, is a greenish yellow **diatomic** gas at room temperature. Chlorine can be prepared in the laboratory by the **oxidation** of hydrochloric acid. Small amounts of chlorine are added to water in swimming pools, and to some water supplies, to kill bacteria. Simple tests may be used to measure the amount of dissolved chlorine. If the **concentration** of chlorine is too high, it can endanger human health – if it is too low, it might not be effective. One important chlorine **compound** is sodium hypochlorite, the main ingredient of domestic bleach. Other halogen compounds include **CFCs** (chlorofluorocarbons). CFCs deplete, or break down, the ozone layer in the upper atmosphere, allowing harmful radiation from the Sun to reach Earth's surface.

POSITION IN THE PERIODIC TABLE

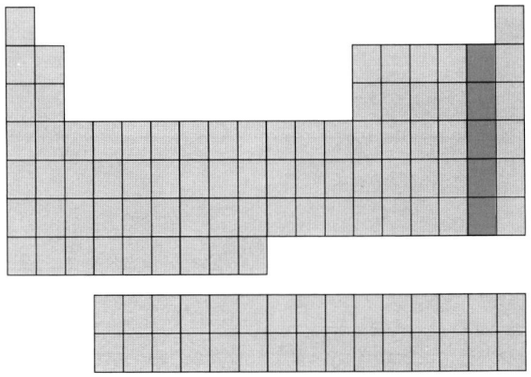

GROUP 17 ELEMENTS
The halogens form group 17 of the periodic table. They are (top to bottom): fluorine (F), chlorine (Cl), bromine (Br), iodine (I), and astatine (At).

PREPARATION OF CHLORINE
Chlorine gas, Cl_2, is prepared in the laboratory by the oxidation of hydrochloric acid, HCl, using manganese(IV) oxide, MnO_2. The chlorine produced contains some water vapor, but is dried by passing it through concentrated sulfuric acid, H_2SO_4. In order to prevent this acid being sucked back into the reaction vessel, an empty dreschel bottle is placed between the acid bottle and the vessel to act as an anti-suck-back device (see p. 23). The dry gas is collected in a gas jar. Chlorine gas is poisonous.

BROMINE AND IODINE
The element bromine is a red liquid at room temperature, though it vaporizes easily, producing a brown vapor. Iodine is a violet solid at room temperature, which sublimes (turns to vapor without passing through a liquid phase) when warmed.

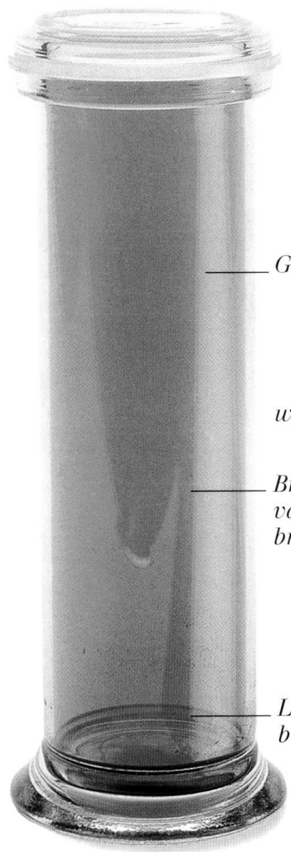

BROMINE

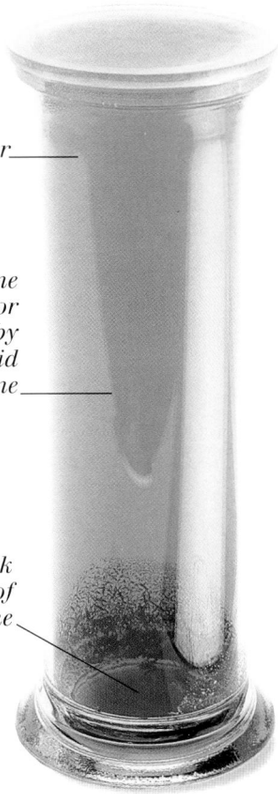

IODINE

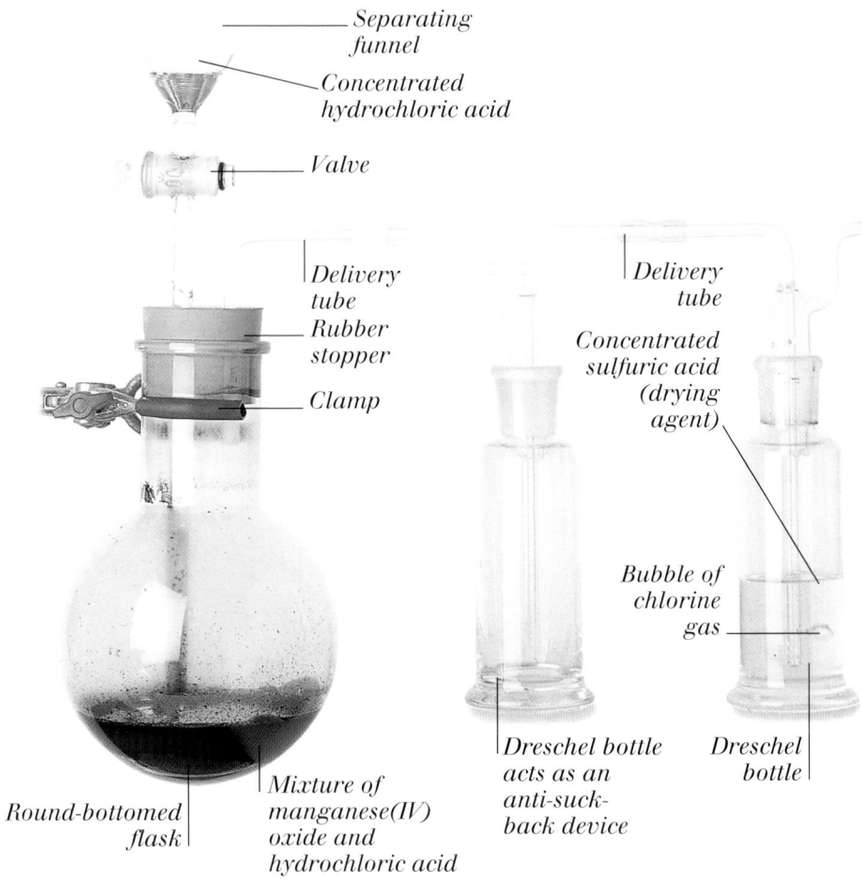

CHLORINE IN WATER

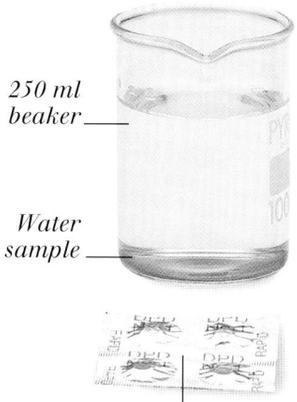

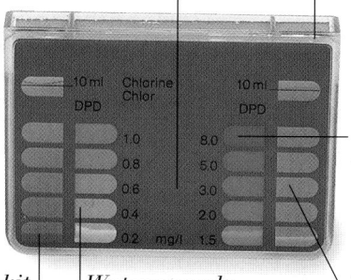

CHLORINE TEST KIT
Water can be tested for its chlorine concentration using kits such as this one. Chlorine in the water forms colored **complex ions** when a tablet is added, and the intensity of the color reveals the chlorine concentration.

BLEACHING

SODIUM HYPOCHLORITE SOLUTION

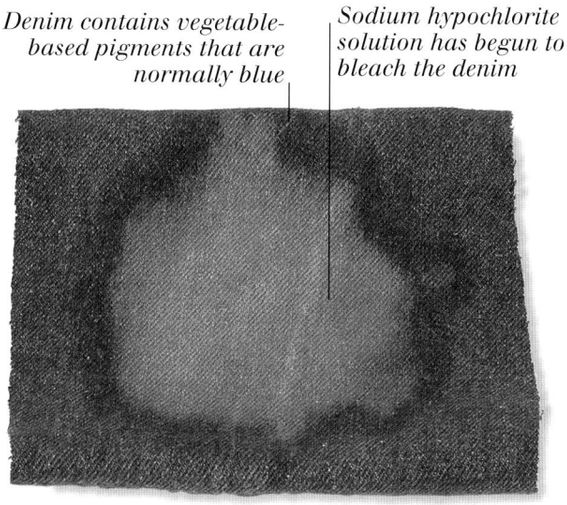

BLEACHING ACTION OF SODIUM HYPOCHLORITE
Sodium hypochlorite, NaOCl, is an industrially important chlorine compound that is a strong oxidizing agent. It bleaches pigments by giving up its oxygen to them, making them colorless.

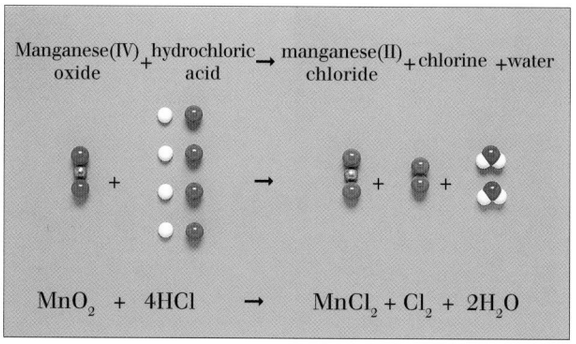

MOLECULAR VIEW
Four units of the hydrochloric acid are oxidized by each **molecule** of manganese(IV) oxide. The manganese(IV) is **reduced** to manganese(II).

OZONE DEPLETION REACTIONS

CFCs, synthetic **organic** compounds containing chlorine and fluorine atoms, have been used in packaging and some aerosol cans. Released into the atmosphere, CFCs lose chlorine atoms. These atoms **catalyze** reactions that damage the ozone layer, which shields Earth from harmful solar radiation.

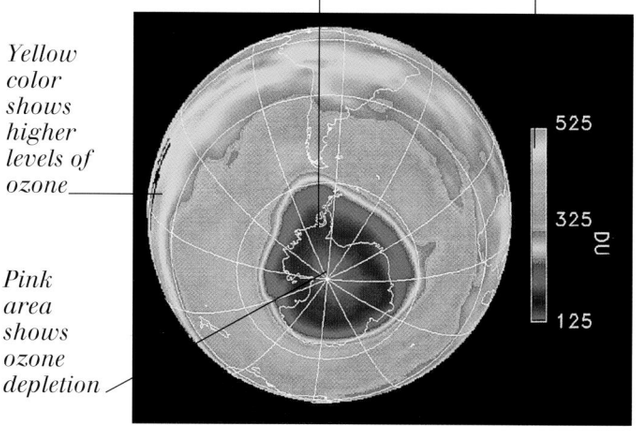

DEPLETION OF THE OZONE LAYER

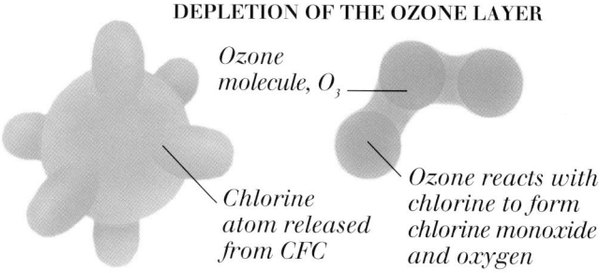

CHLORINE AND OZONE

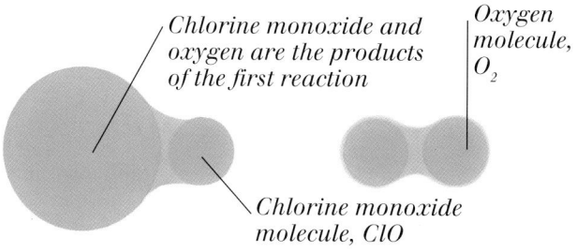

CHLORINE MONOXIDE AND OXYGEN

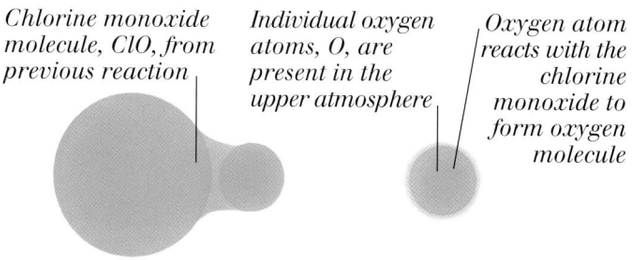

CHLORINE MONOXIDE AND OXYGEN

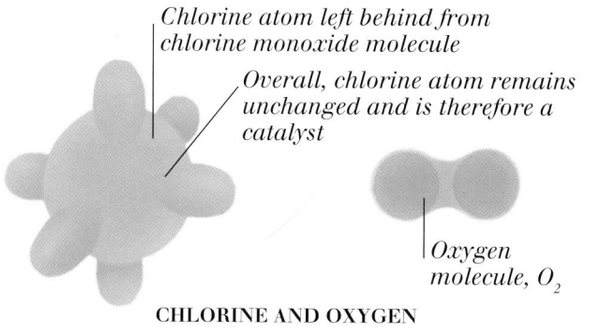

CHLORINE AND OXYGEN

Organic chemistry 1

ORGANIC CHEMISTRY IS THE study of carbon **compounds**, although it normally excludes carbon dioxide and **salts** such as calcium carbonate (see pp. 24–25). There are more carbon-based compounds than compounds based on all the other **elements** put together. This is because carbon **atoms** easily bond to each other, forming long chains and rings that include single bonds, double bonds (see p. 17), and triple bonds. **Hydrocarbons** are **molecules** containing only carbon and hydrogen. There are three main families of hydrocarbons based on carbon chains, called **alkanes**, **alkenes**, and **alkynes** (right). Ethyne is the simplest alkyne, with two carbon atoms. Most carbon compounds occur in different structural forms, or **isomers**. For example, the hydrocarbon butene has two isomers that differ in the position of the double bond. Crude oil is a **mixture** (see pp. 8–9) of long-chain hydrocarbons, which is separated industrially in a fractionating tower, and cracked (heated with a **catalyst**) to produce more useful short-chain compounds.

Particles of soot

Ethyne burns in a flame, producing water vapor and carbon dioxide

Ethyne is a colorless gas

Glass tube

Calcium carbide, CaC_2, is a brown ionic solid

Watch glass

Rubber stopper

Clamp stand

Boiling tube

Clamp

CaC_2 and H_2O become C_2H_2 and $Ca(OH)_2$

PREPARATION OF ETHYNE
Ethyne, C_2H_2, a gas at room temperature, is the simplest alkyne. It is prepared by the **exothermic** reaction of water with calcium carbide, CaC_2. Like all hydrocarbons, ethyne burns to produce water and carbon dioxide. Soot (pure carbon) may be formed due to incomplete burning.

CALCIUM CARBIDE
Calcium carbide, CaC_2, is an **ionic** solid that contains the Ca^{2+} and C_2^{2-} **ions**. In ethyne, the **product** of the reaction, carbon and hydrogen atoms are **covalently bound**.

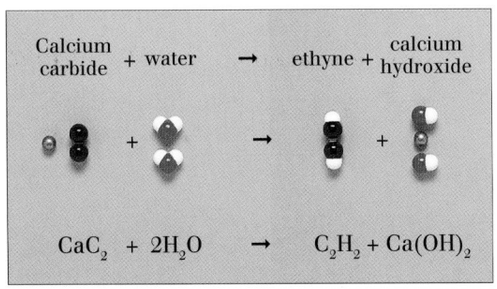

MOLECULAR VIEW
Carbon atoms from calcium carbide combine with hydrogen atoms from water molecules to form ethyne.

FAMILIES OF HYDROCARBONS
Alkanes have only single bonds in the chain of carbon atoms. Alkenes have at least one double bond in the chain, while alkynes have a triple bond.

ALKANES

Tetrahedral shape

Carbon atom

Hydrogen atom

Single bond

METHANE **ETHANE**

Propane has three carbon atoms

Butane has four carbon atoms

PROPANE **BUTANE**

ALKENES

Ethene has two carbon atoms

Double bond

Propene has three carbon atoms

ETHENE **PROPENE**

Double bond is first bond in chain

Butene has two isomers

Butene has four carbon atoms

Double bond is second in chain

BUT-1-ENE **BUT-2-ENE**

ALKYNES

Triple bond

ETHYNE

Propyne exists in one form only

Triple bond

Single bond

PROPYNE

Triple bond is second bond in carbon chain

Butyne has two isomers

BUT-2-YNE

Triple bond is first bond in carbon chain

BUT-1-YNE

CATALYTIC CRACKING OF OIL

Clamp
Cotton
Products may contain pure carbon, deposited on cotton
Rubber stopper
Delivery tube
Crude oil
Catalytic cracking takes place at the surface of the pot pieces
Porous pot pieces
Crude oil is a mixture of hydrocarbons
Bunsen flame heats the oil

CATALYTIC CRACKING
In this laboratory setup, a mixture of long-chain hydrocarbons is vaporized and passed over pieces of porous pot. The long hydrocarbons attach to the pieces and **decompose** into smaller molecules. The pot acts as a catalyst.

Products of cracking are hydrocarbons with shorter chains
Upturned test tube collects gases
Products may include hydrogen gas
Clamp
500 ml beaker
Water

FRACTIONAL DISTILLATION

FRACTIONAL DISTILLATION
Crude oil is made up of a mixture of hydrocarbons. This mixture is separated into fractions (groups of hydrocarbons with similar boiling points) by a process called fractional **distillation.** This process takes place in a fractionating tower. The oil is vaporized, and each fraction condenses to a liquid at a different **temperature.**

Refinery gas escapes at the top of the tower
Condenser
Refinery gas contains methane, ethane, propane, and butane
110°C
Water from condenser
Naphtha (a mixture of hydrocarbons used for many applications) emerges here
150°C
Gasoline (light hydrocarbons used for fuel)
Kerosene (paraffin oil) used as aircraft oil and for domestic heating
190°C
Fractionating tower is typically 40 m tall
Condensed gases (reflux) run down inside of tower
Fractions to be processed for transportation fuel
Furnace
Crude oil vaporizes in furnace
280°C
Steam is pumped in to heat unvaporized oil
300°C
Pump
Some of the residue goes to be cracked (above)
Residue contains long-chain hydrocarbons, including tar for roads and wax for candles

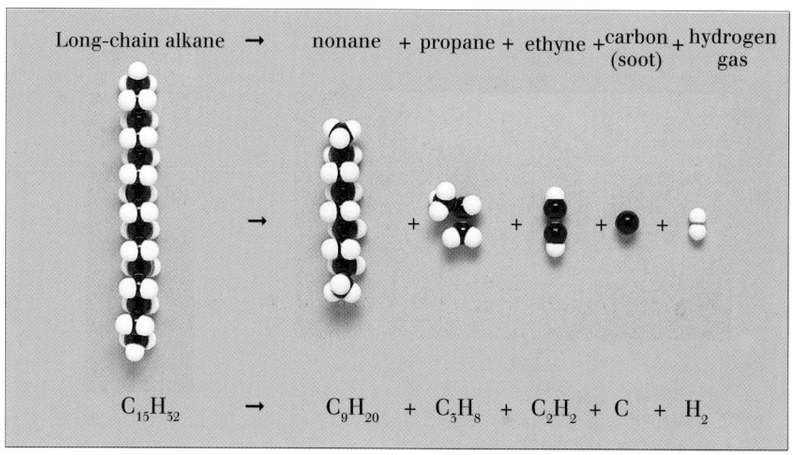

MOLECULAR VIEW
In the catalytic cracking of oil, hydrocarbon chains, shown here as 15 carbon atoms long, break into smaller chains with between 2 and 9 carbons. This is a molecular model of a general reaction. In reality, many other similar reactions are also likely to occur.

Organic chemistry 2

THE CHEMISTRY OF CARBON is called **organic** chemistry. Simple organic **molecules** (see pp. 50–51) are based on chains of carbon **atoms**. Carbon atoms are very versatile at bonding, and can form very large and complicated molecules. Small organic molecules often join together to form larger ones. For example, glucose, a simple sugar or monosaccharide, is a small organic molecule. Two saccharide units join to form a disaccharide, such as sucrose. Large numbers of sugar units can join to form polysaccharides such as starch (see p. 27). The process of joining large numbers of identical molecules together is called **polymerization**. The polymers that result are commonplace both in synthetic products and in nature. Plastics, such as nylon and PVC, are polymers, and much more complicated polymers form the basis of life. Hemoglobin is a large organic molecule responsible for carrying oxygen in red blood cells. DNA is a giant molecule that holds the genetic code in all living organisms. This code is created from patterns of four small molecules called bases, which are arranged along the famous double helix structure.

SUCROSE CRYSTALS

Sugars are **carbohydrates**. Sucrose (see p. 27) is the chemical name for ordinary household sugar. In this beaker, **crystals** of sucrose have formed from an **aqueous solution** of household sugar.

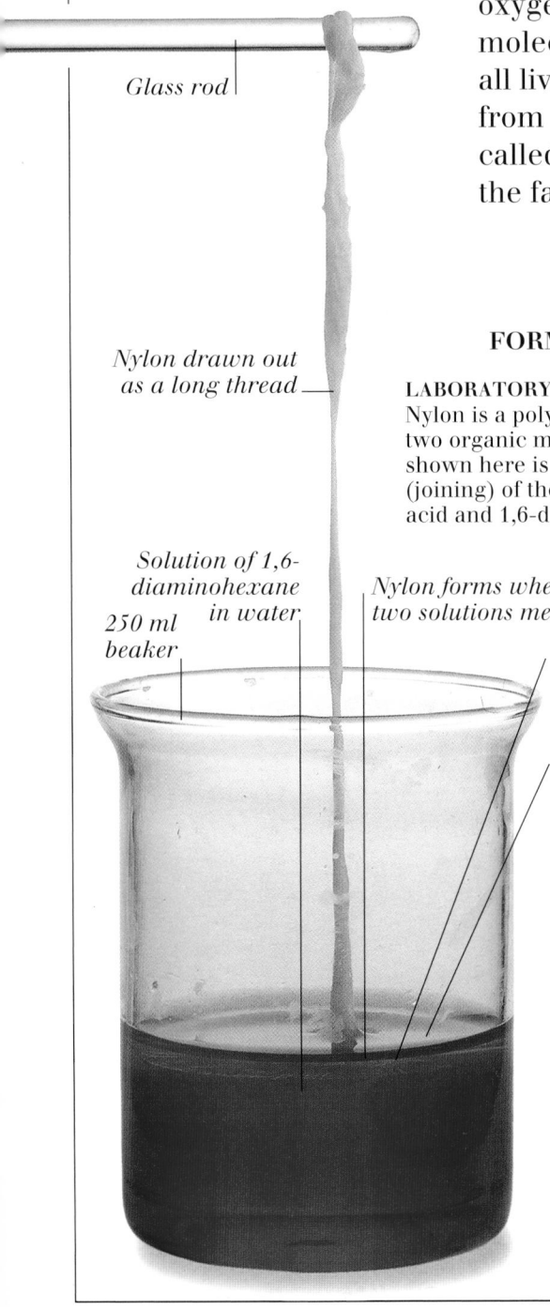

FORMATION OF NYLON

LABORATORY PREPARATION
Nylon is a polymer that is formed from two organic monomers. The form of nylon shown here is made by the synthesis (joining) of the monomers hexanedioic acid and 1,6-diaminohexane.

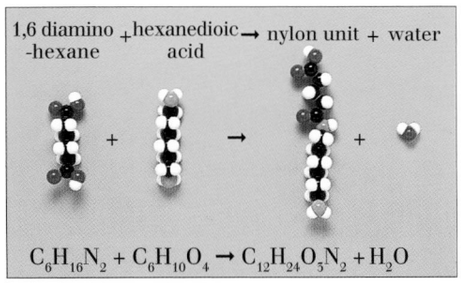

MOLECULAR VIEW
A unit of nylon is made from one molecule of each monomer (above). Each unit reacts again with one monomer at each end, eventually forming the polymer nylon. A nylon molecule may comprise hundreds of such units.

PLASTICS

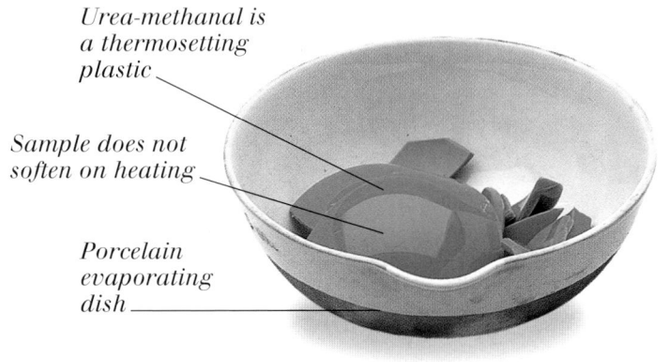

THERMOSETTING PLASTICS
Thermosetting plastics are molded when first made, and harden upon cooling. They cannot be softened again by heating.

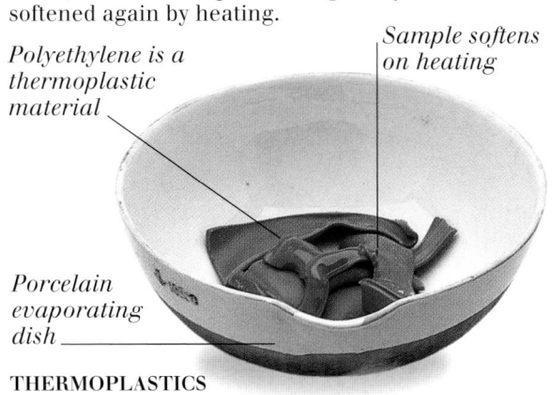

THERMOPLASTICS
Some plastics soften on heating. They can be remolded while hot, then allowed to cool and harden. Polyethylene is an example of such a thermoplastic.

POLYMERIZATION

CHLOROETHENE
Molecules of chloroethene are identical to those of ethene (see p. 50), except that they have a chlorine atom in place of one of the hydrogen atoms. Each molecule contains one double bond.

POLY(CHLOROETHENE), PVC
Chloroethene molecules are the monomers that form the polymer poly(chloroethene), also known as PVC (derived from polyvinylchloride, an older name). The double bond in each monomer breaks as the molecules join together.

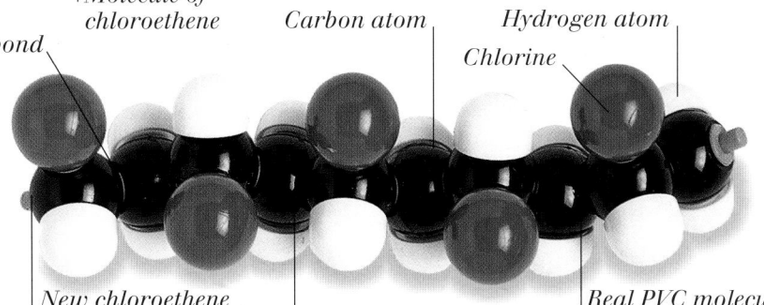

BIOCHEMISTRY

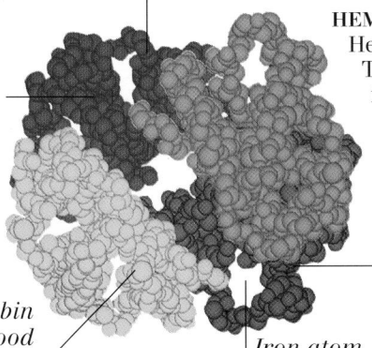

HEMOGLOBIN
Hemoglobin carries oxygen in blood. This computer image shows the framework of the hemoglobin molecule, which consists of four **proteins**. One iron atom is associated with each protein, and each iron atom can hold one oxygen molecule.

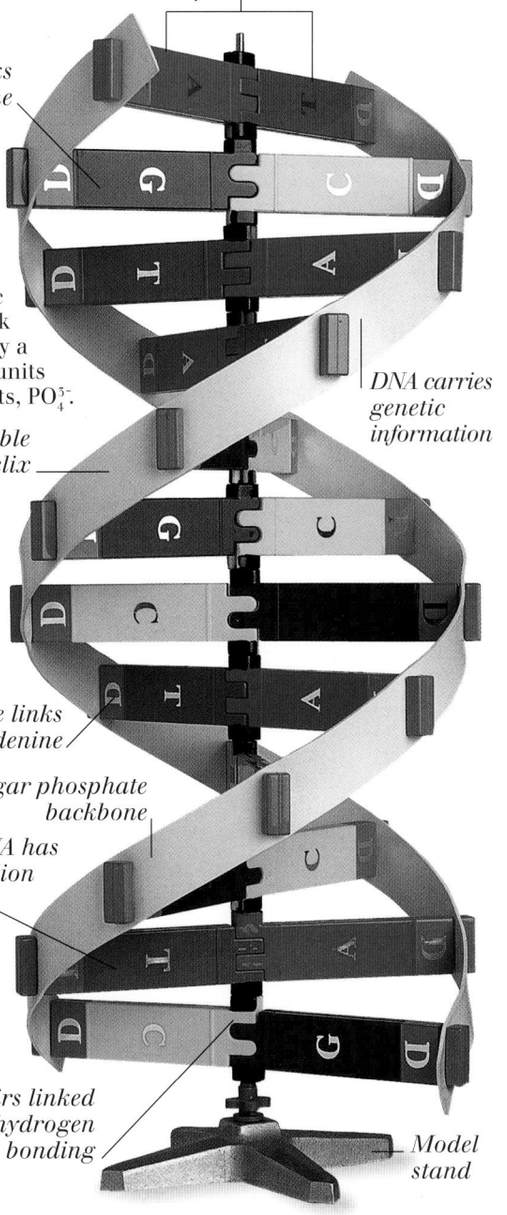

MODEL OF DNA STRUCTURE
This model shows the double helix structure of DNA (deoxyribonucleic acid). Pairs of the bases (below) link together, and are held in place by a backbone of sugar units bonded to phosphate units, PO_4^{3-}.

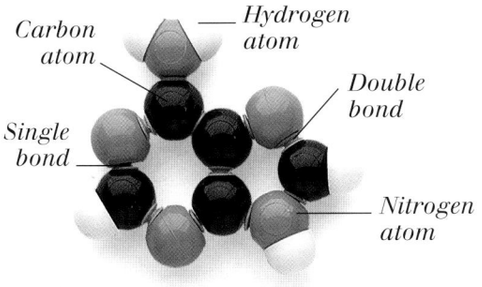

ADENINE
One of the four bases in the structure of DNA is adenine. It contains only carbon, hydrogen, and nitrogen atoms.

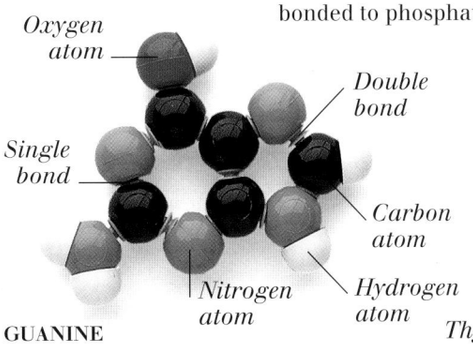

GUANINE
Guanine is the base that links with cytosine in DNA. Links are made at two points in each molecule.

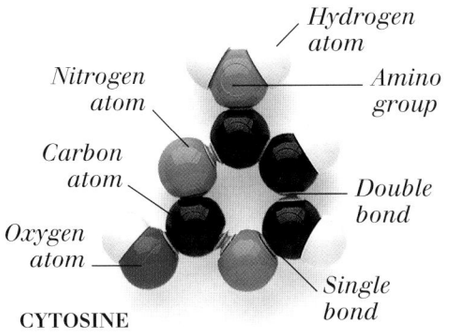

CYTOSINE
The cytosine molecule consists of a ring, with an oxygen and an amino group ($-NH_2$) attached.

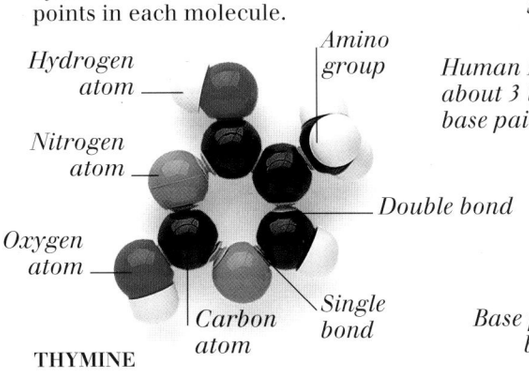

THYMINE
The base that links with adenine in DNA is thymine. Links are made at two points in each molecule.

Chemical analysis

THERE ARE MANY SITUATIONS, from geological surveys to forensic investigations, that call for the chemical analysis of unknown substances. The substances being analyzed may be present only in tiny amounts, and may be **mixtures** of many different **compounds**. Separation techniques such as **chromatography** (see pp. 8–9) are often the starting point in an analysis. Simple laboratory tests may follow – these normally identify one part of a compound at a time. For example, flame tests are used to identify **cations** of metallic **elements** in a compound, and **radicals** may be identified by heating the compound to **decompose** it, thereby releasing signifying gases. Many simple laboratory tests are performed on **aqueous solutions** of the unknown substance. The substance is crushed and dissolved in water, and other **solutions**, such as ammonium hydroxide or silver nitrate, are added. The color of any **precipitate** formed indicates the presence of a specific **ion**. In contrast, mass **spectrometry** is a highly complex but very powerful testing technique. The sample to be tested is vaporized, then ionized. The ions are separated by a strong magnetic field and identified according to their **electric charge** and mass.

FLAME TEST

A sample of an unknown compound is held on the end of a platinum wire in a Bunsen burner flame. Specific colors in the flame indicate the presence of certain metals.

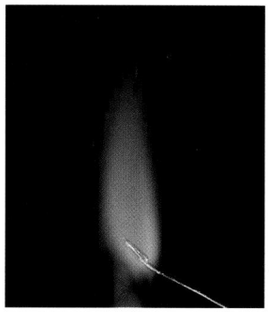

Flame turns bluish white

Flame turns orange-red

CALCIUM
Compounds of calcium turn the flame orange-red.

LEAD
Lead **salts** give the flame a bluish white color.

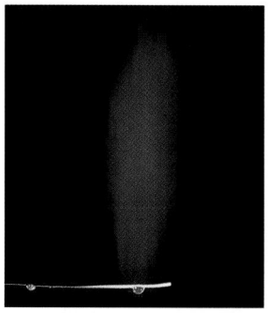

Flame turns yellow-green

Flame turns pale violet

POTASSIUM
Compounds of potassium turn the flame pale violet.

BARIUM
Barium salts turn the flame yellow-green.

TEST FOR A CARBONATE OR HYDROGENCARBONATE

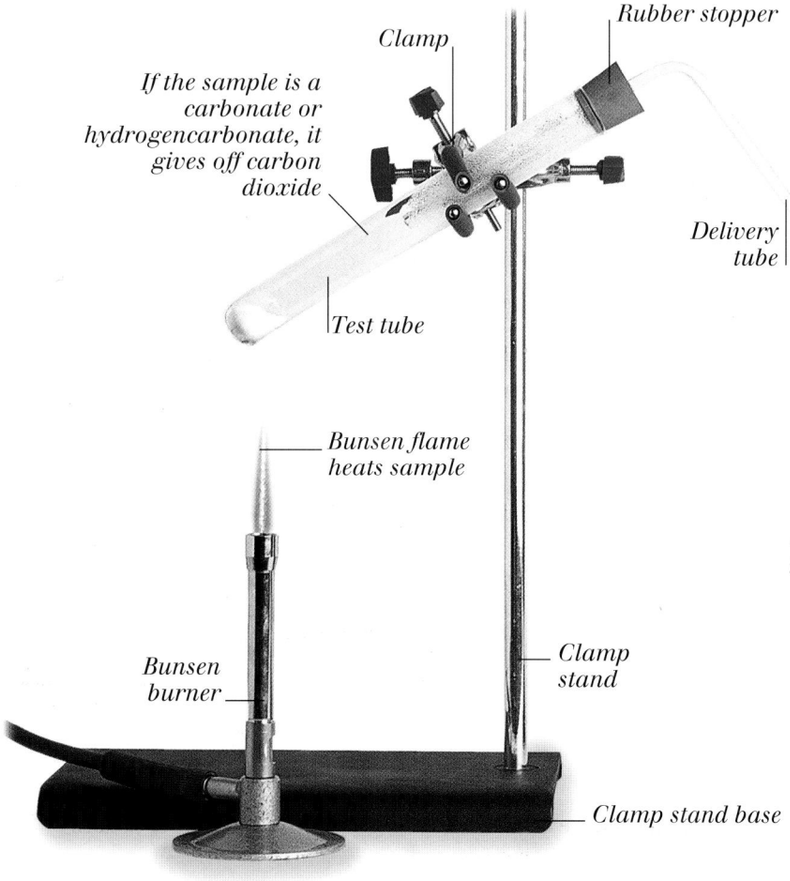

HEATING THE COMPOUND

A carbonate is a compound containing the carbonate radical, CO_3^{2-} – for example, calcium carbonate (see pp. 24–25 and 38–39). A hydrogencarbonate contains the hydrogencarbonate radical, HCO_3^-. When heated, these radicals give off carbon dioxide gas, which can be identified by bubbling it through limewater (a solution of calcium hydroxide).

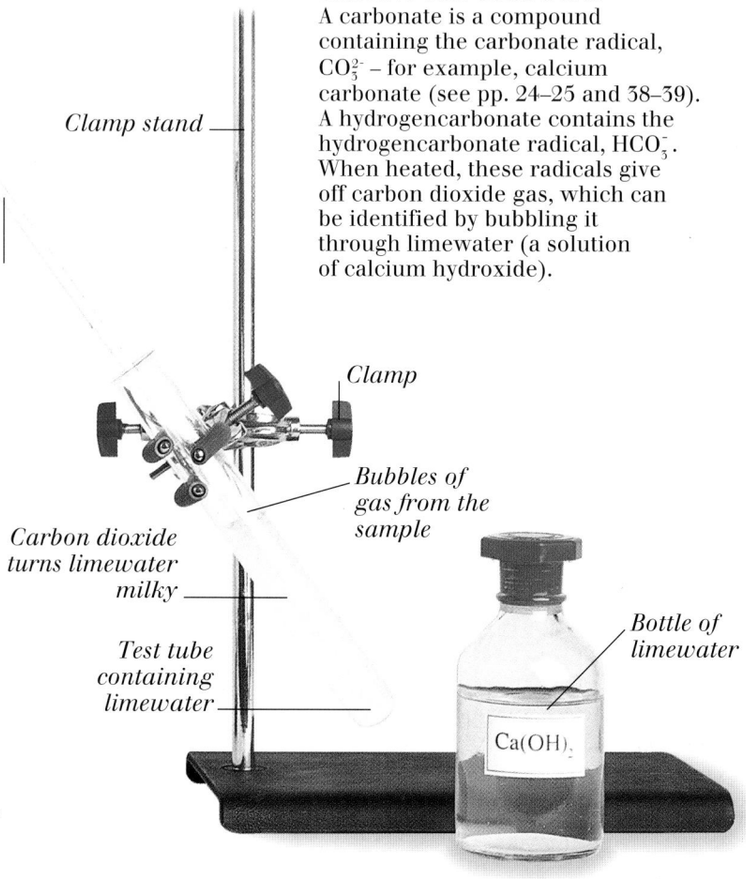

TESTING FOR CATIONS

ACTION OF AMMONIUM HYDROXIDE
Many different tests are used to identify **cations** in an unknown compound. One simple test is carried out on a pure solution of the unknown compound in water. A dilute solution of ammonium hydroxide, NH_4OH, is added to the test solution. If a gelatinous precipitate forms, any cations present can often be identified by the color of the precipitate.

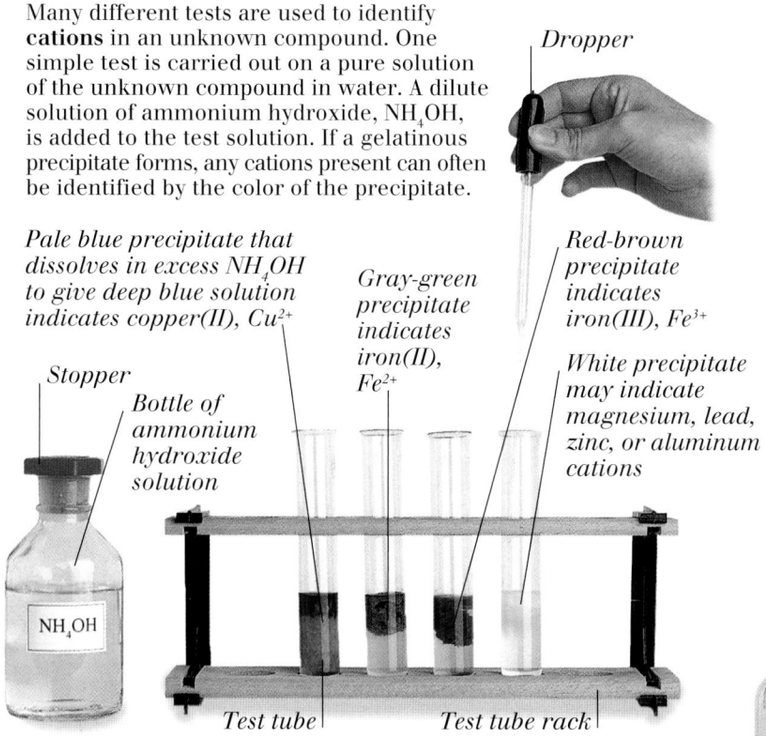

TEST RESULTS
A few solutions have been tested, and precipitates have formed in the test tubes. From the colors of the precipitates, the metal cations present in the samples have been identified.

MASS SPECTROMETER

In a mass spectrometer, the sample to be tested is vaporized, then converted into ions and shot into a curved tube. A magnetic field in the tube deflects those ions with a specific mass and charge into a detector. Changing the magnetic field strength allows a mass spectrum – an analysis of all the ions present – to be built up, from which the the test substance can be accurately identified.

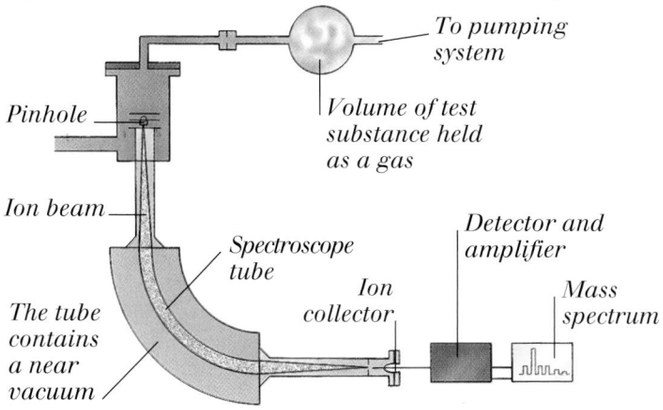

TESTING FOR ANIONS

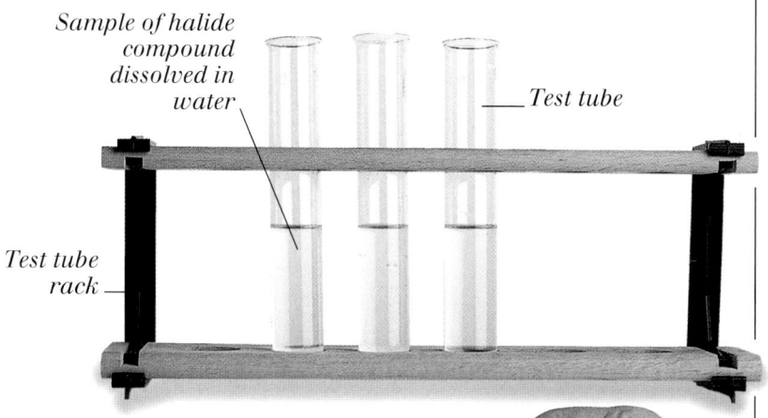

ACTION OF SILVER NITRATE SOLUTION
Of the many different tests used to identify **anions** in an unknown compound, the addition of aqueous silver nitrate, $AgNO_3$, to an aqueous solution of the compound is often the first step. If halide ions – ions of the halogens (see pp. 48–49) – are present in solution, a colored precipitate forms.

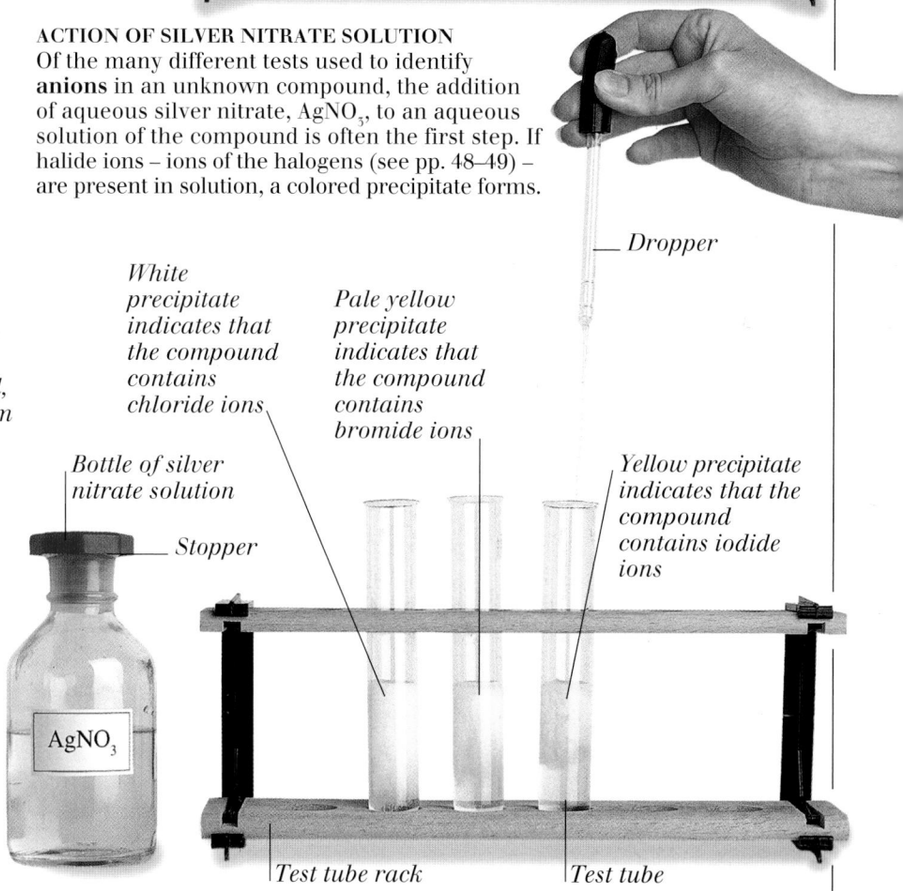

TEST RESULTS
Here, solutions of compounds containing ions of the halogens chlorine, iodine, and bromine have been tested. Salts containing ions of the halogens are called halides. Precipitates have formed in the test tubes.

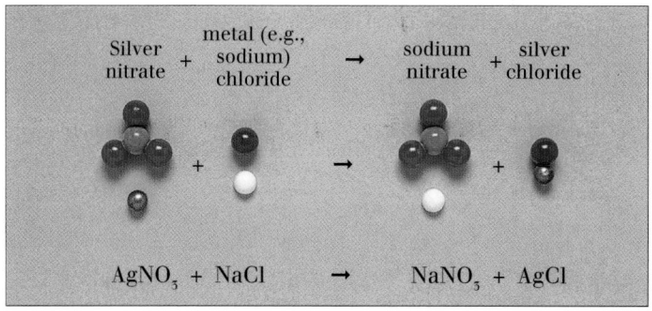

MOLECULAR VIEW OF REACTION
A **double decomposition reaction** takes place between silver nitrate and the halide salt in solution, and insoluble silver halides form. Silver halides are used in photography (see p. 26).

Useful data

IMPORTANT IONS AND RADICALS

NAME	FORMULA AND CHARGE
Hydrogen	H^+
Sodium	Na^+
Potassium	K^+
Magnesium	Mg^{2+}
Calcium	Ca^{2+}
Aluminum	Al^{3+}
Iron(II)	Fe^{2+}
Iron(III)	Fe^{3+}
Copper(I)	Cu^+
Copper(II)	Cu^{2+}
Silver(I)	Ag^+
Zinc	Zn^{2+}
Ammonium	NH^{4+}
Hydronium	H_3O^+
Oxide	O^{2-}
Sulfide	S^{2-}
Fluoride	F^-
Chloride	Cl^-
Bromide	Br^-
Iodide	I^-
Hydroxide	OH^-
Carbonate	CO_3^{2-}
Hydrogencarbonate	HCO_3^-
Nitrate(V)	NO_3^-
Sulfate(VI)	SO_4^{2-}

COMMON NAMES AND FORMULAE OF IMPORTANT COMPOUNDS

COMMON NAME	CHEMICAL NAME	FORMULA
Water	Hydrogen oxide	H_2O
Salt	Sodium chloride	$NaCl$
Sodium bicarbonate	Sodium hydrogencarbonate	$NaHCO_3$
Washing soda	Sodium carbonate decahydrate	$Na_2CO_3.10H_2O$
Household bleach	Sodium hypochlorite	$NaOCl$
Methylated spirits	Methanol	CH_3OH
Alcohol	Ethanol	C_2H_5OH
Vinegar	Ethanoic acid	$CH_3.COOH$
Vitamin C	Ascorbic acid	$C_4H_3O_4.CHOH.CH_2OH$
Aspirin	Acetylsalicylic acid	$C_6H_4.COOCH_3.COOH$
White sugar	Sucrose	$C_6H_{11}O_5.O.C_6H_{11}O_5$
Limestone/chalk	Calcium carbonate	$CaCO_3$
Plaster of Paris	Calcium sulfate hemihydrate	$CaSO_4.\frac{1}{2}H_2O$
Rust	Hydrated iron(III) oxide	$Fe_2O_3.xH_2O$*

**Exact number of water molecules varies.*

NAMES AND STRUCTURES OF COMMON PLASTICS

COMMON NAME OF PLASTIC	PROPER NAME	REPEATED UNIT (MONOMER)
Polyethylene	Poly(ethene)	Ethene, C_2H_4
PVC or polyvinylchloride	Poly(chloroethene)	Chloroethene, C_2H_3Cl
Polystyrene	Poly(phenylethene)	Phenylethene, $C_2H_3.C_6H_5$
Acrylic	Poly(propenonitrile)	Propenonitrile, $C_2H_2.CH_3.CN$
PTFE or Teflon®	Poly(tetrafluoroethene)	Tetrafluoroethene, C_2F_4

DISCOVERY OF ELEMENTS

ELEMENT NAME	DISCOVERED*	ORIGIN OF NAME
Carbon, C	known since ancient times	Latin *carbo*, charcoal
Gold, Au	known since ancient times	Old English *geolo*, yellow; Latin *aurum*, gold
Sulfur, S	known since ancient times	Latin *sulfur*, brimstone
Platinum, Pt	16th century	Spanish *platina*, little silver
Cobalt, Co	1735 by Georg Brandt	German *kobold*, goblin
Hydrogen, H	1766 by Henry Cavendish	Greek *hydro-* and *genes*, water-maker
Chlorine, Cl	1774 by Carl Wilhelm Scheele	Greek *chloros*, greenish yellow
Tungsten, W	1783 by Juan José and Fausto Elhuyar	Swedish *tung*, heavy, and *sten*, stone; German *wolfram*
Chromium, Cr	1797 by Louis-Nicolas Vauquelin	Greek *chroma*, color
Bromine, Br	1826 by Antoine-Jérôme Balard	Greek *bromos*, stench
Helium, He	1868 by Pierre Janssen and Joseph Norman Lockyer	Greek *helios*, the Sun
Unnilquadium, Unq	1964 (in USSR) and 1969 (in US)	Latin for 104, the element's atomic number**

** Generally refers to when the pure substance was first isolated – its recognition as an element often came later.*
*** Because of disputes over the discovery of elements with atomic numbers 104–109, their names are yet to be finalized.*

MELTING AND BOILING POINTS OF SOME ELEMENTS

ELEMENT	MELTING POINT °C	MELTING POINT °F	BOILING POINT °C	BOILING POINT °F
Mercury	-39	-38	357	675
Helium	-272	-458	-269	-452
Tungsten	3,410	6,170	5,555	10,031
Nitrogen	-210	-346	-196	-321
Sodium	98	208	883	1,621
Oxygen	-219	-362	-183	-297
Bromine	-7	19	59	138
Iron	1,535	2,795	2,862	5,184
Carbon	3,550	6,420	4,827	8,720
Gold	1,063	1,945	2,970	5,379

THE MOST ABUNDANT ELEMENTS IN THE EARTH'S CRUST

ELEMENT	MASS (%)
Oxygen	49.13
Silicon	26.00
Aluminum	7.45
Iron	4.20
Calcium	3.25
Sodium	2.40
Potassium	2.35
Magnesium	2.35
Hydrogen	1.00
Others	1.87

Glossary

ACID: A **compound** containing hydrogen that can donate **protons** (hydrogen **ions**, H^+). In **aqueous solution**, the protons associate with water **molecules** to form **hydronium ions**, H_3O^+.

ACTIVATION ENERGY: The least **energy** required for a particular **chemical reaction** to take place. Typically, it is supplied as heat energy – striking a match produces heat to start the match **burning**.

ALKALI: A **base** that is soluble in water. When it dissolves, it produces hydroxide **ions**, OH^-.

ALKANE: A **hydrocarbon** that has only single bonds between its carbon **atoms** – for example, ethane.

ALKENE: A **hydrocarbon** such as ethene that has one or more double bonds between its carbon **atoms**.

ALKYNE: A **hydrocarbon** such as propyne that has one or more triple bonds between its carbon **atoms**.

ALLOTROPES: Forms of the same **element** with different **molecular** or **crystalline** structures. Diamond and graphite are allotropes of carbon.

ALLOY: A **mixture** of a metal with other metals or nonmetals in certain proportions, prepared when they are molten. Bronze is an alloy of the metals copper and tin, while steel is an alloy of iron and the nonmetal carbon.

ANHYDROUS: Describing a substance that has lost its **water of crystallization**. Adding water rehydrates an anhydrous substance.

ANION: An **ion** or **radical** with a negative **electric charge** – for example, the fluoride ion, F^-, and the sulfate radical, SO_4^{2-}. Anions are attracted to the **anode** during **electrolysis**.

ANODE: In an **electrochemical cell**, the **electrode** where **oxidation** occurs. The anode is the positive terminal in an electrolytic cell, but negative in a voltaic cell.

RHOMBIC (α) SULFUR CRYSTALS

AQUEOUS SOLUTION: A **solution** in which the **solvent** is water.

ATOM: The smallest part of an **element** that retains its chemical identity. Overall electrically neutral, atoms consist of negatively charged **electrons** that surround a central, positively charged **nucleus**.

ATOMIC FORCE MICROSCOPE: A device used to produce images of **atoms**, which even very powerful light microscopes cannot resolve. A probe scans a solid surface, closely following its contours. A computer converts the probe's motion into an image of the surface atoms.

ATOMIC NUMBER: The number of **protons** in the **nucleus** of an **atom**, which is unique to each **element**.

BASE: A **compound** that can accept **protons** (hydrogen **ions**, H^+) to neutralize **acids**, producing a **salt** and water.

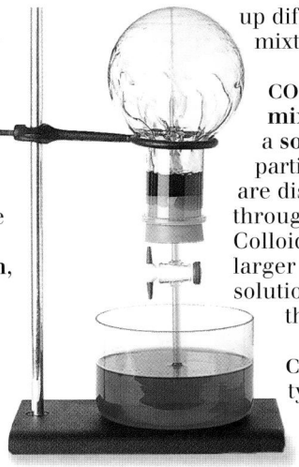

AQUEOUS SOLUTION OF AMMONIA

BURNING: Also called combustion, burning is the rapid combination of a substance with oxygen. It is an **exothermic** reaction.

CARBOHYDRATE: An **organic compound**, such as a sugar, that contains the **elements** carbon, hydrogen, and oxygen only.

CATALYST: A substance that increases the **rate** of a **chemical reaction**, but is itself unchanged at the end of the reaction.

CATHODE: In an **electrochemical cell**, the **electrode** where **reduction** occurs. The cathode is the negative terminal in an electrolytic cell, but the positive one in a voltaic cell.

CATION: An **ion** or **radical** with a positive **electric charge**. Metals readily form cations, such as the copper(II) ion, Cu^{2+}. Cations are attracted to the **cathode** during **electrolysis**.

CFC: Abbreviation for chlorofluorocarbon. Any **compound** formed by replacing some or all of the hydrogen **atoms** of a **hydrocarbon** with chlorine and fluorine atoms. CFCs released in the atmosphere attack the ozone layer.

CHEMICAL REACTION: A process in which **elements** or **compounds** (the **reactants**) change to form different elements or compounds (the **products**). The change may be permanent or reversible. During a chemical reaction, **electrons** are transferred or shared between the reactants.

CHROMATOGRAPHY: A technique used to separate a **mixture**. The various types of chromatography all use a substance (known as the stationary phase) that takes up different parts of the mixture at different rates.

COLLOID: A type of **mixture**, similar to a **solution**, in which particles of one substance are distributed evenly throughout another. Colloidal particles are larger than those in a solution, but smaller than those in a **suspension**.

COMPLEX ION: A type of **ion** in which a central metallic **cation** is combined with surrounding **anions** or **molecules**. Iron and other **transition metals** form complex ions with water molecules.

COMPOUND: A pure substance in which **elements** are chemically combined in a definite ratio. In the compound water, H_2O, **atoms** of hydrogen and oxygen are bound together in the ratio 2:1. Compounds with **covalent bonding** generally consist of **molecules**. When solid, compounds with **ionic bonding** consist of **macromolecules**.

CONCENTRATION: The amount of a dissolved substance (**solute**) present in unit volume of **solution**. The molar concentration has units of **moles** per liter (mol l^{-1}), while the units of mass concentration are kilograms per liter (kg l^{-1}).

COVALENT BONDING: A type of chemical bonding in which **electrons** are shared between the **atoms** involved. **Compounds** that exhibit this type of bonding are called covalent compounds.

CRYSTAL: A regular arrangement of **atoms**, **ions**, or **molecules** in a solid. This regular internal structure leads to a geometrically regular external shape. Sodium chloride crystals, for example, are cubic.

REHYDRATING ANHYDROUS CRYSTALS

DECOMPOSITION: Any **chemical reaction** in which a **compound** breaks down into simpler compounds or **elements**. Many compounds decompose upon heating or **electrolysis**.

DEHYDRATING AGENT: Removes water from another substance in a **chemical reaction** called dehydration. Some dehydrating agents can remove hydrogen and oxygen in the ratio 2:1 to make water where there was none before.

DIATOMIC: Describing a **molecule** that is made up of two **atoms**. Hydrogen is a diatomic gas.

DISPLACEMENT REACTION: A **chemical reaction** in which one **atom**, **ion**, or **molecule** replaces another. Zinc displaces copper from a **solution** of copper(II) ions, Cu^{2+}.

DISTILLATION: Boiling a liquid to vaporize it, and then condensing the vapor back into a liquid in a separate vessel. Distillation is used to separate the **solute** from the **solvent** in a **solution**. A **mixture** of liquids with different boiling points is separated by fractional distillation.

DOUBLE DECOMPOSITION: A **chemical reaction** between two **salts** in which **ions** or **radicals** are exchanged, usually in **solution**.

EFFLORESCENT: Describing a substance that loses some or all of its **water of crystallization** to the air, forming a new, often powdery substance. If all the water is lost, the **anhydrous** form results.

ELECTRIC CHARGE: The property of a particle that gives rise to the electrostatic forces responsible for chemical activity, and for holding **atoms** together. Charge can be negative or positive. Like charges repel, and unlike charges attract.

ELECTROCHEMICAL CELL: A system consisting of an **electrolyte**, two **electrodes** (a **cathode** and an **anode**), and an external electric circuit. There are two basic types of electrochemical cells: electrolytic cells, used in **electrolysis** and electroplating, and voltaic cells, as found in household batteries.

ELECTRODE: A plate made from an electrical conductor, sometimes graphite but usually metal, for use in **electrochemical cells**. In a cell, one electrode is the **anode**, and the other is the **cathode**.

ELECTROLYSIS: A process in which a **chemical reaction** occurs as a result of electric current being passed through an **electrolyte**. **Decomposition** of **compounds** can be achieved by electrolysis.

ELECTROLYTE: A paste, liquid, or **solution** containing **ions** that conducts an electric current. The current is carried by **electrically charged** ions, which move toward the oppositely charged **electrode**. Sodium chloride solution and molten sodium chloride are both electrolytes.

ELECTRON: A particle carrying a negative **electric charge** that is found in all **atoms**. In a neutral atom, there are equal numbers of **protons** and electrons.

ELECTRON SHELL: A set of **orbitals** in an **atom**, where **electrons** may be found. The first shell, closest to the **nucleus**, holds up to two electrons in an s-orbital. The second shell has one s- and three p-orbitals, holding up to eight electrons, while the third shell, which also has five d-orbitals, can hold up to 18. Usually, shells are filled progressively from the first shell outward. Across a period, from group 1 through group 18, empty orbitals up to the current shell are filled. Moving from a group 18 **element** to the next (group 1) element, a new shell is begun.

PREPARATION OF NITROGEN DIOXIDE GAS

ELECTROPLATING: A process in which metal **cations** from an **electrolyte** are deposited as a thin layer onto the surface of a metal object that has been made the **cathode**. Many items, from spoons to car bodies, are electroplated.

ELEMENT: A substance containing **atoms** with the same **atomic number**. Every element has characteristic chemical properties. There are 92 naturally occurring elements on Earth.

ENDOTHERMIC: Describing a **chemical reaction** during which heat **energy** is taken in from the surroundings and converted to chemical energy. Endothermic reactions are usually accompanied by a drop in **temperature** of the substances and apparatus.

ENERGY: The ability to make something happen. Energy must be expended in order to do work. Although the total amount of energy in the universe is constant, it can take many interchangeable forms. The two basic forms of energy are potential energy and **kinetic energy**. Potential energy is that energy stored in a system, while kinetic energy is the energy it possesses due to its motion. For example, a nitrogen gas **molecule** in air has potential energy stored in the bond between its **atoms**, and kinetic energy due to its motion through the atmosphere. The potential energy stored in systems made up of atoms, **ions**, and molecules is called chemical energy. During **electrolysis**, electrical energy can be used to overcome this chemical energy to **decompose** molecules.

COPPER CHLORIDE CRYSTALS

ENZYME: A **catalyst** found in, or derived from, a living organism that increases the **rate** of a **chemical reaction**. Enzymes are highly specific, usually catalyzing a particular step in a long and complex chain of reactions. Nearly all enzymes are **proteins**.

EQUILIBRIUM: A stable state in a **reversible reaction**. Such a reaction can be thought of as two simultaneous reactions (the forward and reverse reactions). The reactions are in equilibrium when they proceed at the same **rate**, so that there is no overall change. The equilibrium position determines the proportion of **reactants** to **products** in the reaction vessel.

EXOTHERMIC: Describing a **chemical reaction** during which chemical **energy** of the **reactants** is converted to heat energy and given off to the surroundings. Exothermic reactions are generally accompanied by a rise in **temperature**.

FILTRATION: A method for separating **suspensions**. The suspension is passed through a filter, often made of paper, which is perforated with tiny holes. The holes allow only small **molecules** through, while the larger suspended particles are retained by the filter.

HYBRIDIZATION: The averaging out of bonding **orbital** energies in an **atom**. For example, in carbon atoms as found in diamond, each carbon is joined to four others with bonds of equal **energy**. Each carbon atom normally has one s- and three p-orbitals used for bonding. In diamond, these two types of orbital are converted into four sp^3 hybrid orbitals, each with the same energy.

HYDROCARBON: A **compound** containing the **elements** carbon and hydrogen only. Hydrocarbons are classed as **organic** compounds.

HYDROGEN BONDING: Weak bonding between some **molecules** that contain hydrogen **atoms**, caused by the uneven distribution of **electric charge** within the molecules. Hydrogen bonding is found in water, and is responsible for its relatively high boiling point.

HYDRONIUM ION: This is an **ion** with the formula H_3O^+, which consists of a **proton** or hydrogen ion, H^+, associated with a water **molecule**, H_2O. Hydronium ions form in equal numbers with hydroxide ions, OH^-, when water splits into ions. In a **solution** of an **acid**, there is a greater concentration of H_3O^+ than OH^-, while the opposite is true of an **alkaline** solution. The **concentration** of hydronium ions in solution is given by the **pH** value of the solution.

HYGROSCOPIC: Describing a substance that absorbs water from the air.

INDICATOR: A substance, usually based on natural plant material, whose color changes according to the **acidity** or **alkalinity** of its environment. When added to the test **solution**, **complex ions** of different colors form according to the **pH**. Indicators such as litmus solution and universal indicator are used in chemical analysis.

EXOTHERMIC BURNING REACTION

ION: A particle with **electric charge**, formed when an **atom** gains or loses **electrons**. A positive ion is called a **cation**, and a negative ion is an **anion**.

IONIC BONDING: A type of bonding in which **cations** and **anions** are held together by forces due to their **electric charges**. The **ions** form a **crystal** structure called a **macromolecule**. **Compounds** that contain such bonds are called ionic compounds.

ISOTOPE: One of the possible forms of an **element** that differ in their **nuclear** structure. Although all **atoms** of a particular element have the same number of **protons** in the nucleus, different numbers of **neutrons** can be present. Different isotopes of an element have the same chemical properties, but different **RAMs**. The element fluorine has four isotopes: fluorine-17 (with nine protons and eight neutrons), fluorine-18, fluorine-19, and fluorine-20 (with 11 neutrons).

KINETIC ENERGY: The **energy** that a particle or an object possesses due to its motion or vibration. The more mass an object has and the faster it moves, the more kinetic energy it possesses. Heat energy is the kinetic energy of the random motion of the **atoms**, **ions**, and **molecules** that make up matter.

MACROMOLECULE: Any molecule with an **RMM** greater than about 10,000. The term is often used to refer to **ionic crystals**, such as those of sodium chloride.

MIXTURE: Two or more pure substances (**elements** or **compounds**) that are mixed but not chemically combined. The components of a mixture can be separated by methods such as **chromatography** and **filtration**.

BUCKMINSTERFULLERENE

Solutions and **colloids** are two types of mixtures.

MOLE: A unit of the amount of a substance, defined in terms of the number of particles present. One mole of a substance contains 6.02 x 10^{23} particles, and has a mass in grams equal to its **RAM** or **RMM** – so the mass of one mole of copper is 64.4 grams. The quantity 6.02 x 10^{23} mol^{-1} is Avogadro's constant.

MOLECULAR ORBITAL: A region within a **molecule** in which the **electrons** involved in **covalent bonding** are likely to be found. Molecular orbitals are formed by the overlap of the outer **orbitals** of the **atoms** that are bound together.

MOLECULE: The smallest unit of many **compounds**. It consists of two or more **atoms** held together by **covalent bonding**.

NEUTRON: A particle with no **electric charge** that is found in the **nucleus** of every **atom**, except those of the common **isotope** of hydrogen.

NOBLE GASES: The **elements** of group 18 of the periodic table. These elements are all gases at room temperature, and are very unreactive because they have filled outer **electron shells**.

NUCLEUS: The central, positively charged part of an **atom**, made up of **protons** and **neutrons**. The common **isotope** of hydrogen is the only type of atom that does not have neutrons in its nucleus.

ORBITAL: The region of space around an **atom**, an **ion**, or a **molecule** where **electrons** are likely to be found. In modern theory, electrons are seen to have only a probability of being in a particular region, and not to follow definite orbits. In an atom, the simpler types of orbitals are called s-, p-, and d-orbitals. Atomic orbitals hold up to two electrons each.

ORE: A mineral containing metal **atoms**, normally combined with atoms of oxygen or other **elements**.

ORGANIC: Describing a **compound** based on chains or rings formed by carbon **atoms**. These compounds are the basis of life as we know it. Organic chemistry is the study of such compounds.

OXIDATION: The removal of **electrons** from, or the addition of oxygen to, an **atom**, an **ion**, or a **molecule**. An **element** that is oxidized increases its **oxidation number**.

OXIDATION NUMBER: A positive or negative number that indicates whether an **element** has lost or gained **electrons** during a **chemical reaction.** When copper **atoms** lose two electrons to form doubly charged copper(II) ions, Cu^{2+}, the oxidation number of copper (initially 0) becomes +2, also given by the Roman numeral (II).

pH SCALE: A scale that indicates whether a **solution** is **acidic** or **alkaline**. The scale runs from 1 (strong acid), through 7 (neutral), to 14 (strong alkali). The pH value relates directly to the **concentration** of hydrogen **ions** in the **solution**.

PHOTOSYNTHESIS: A **chemical reaction** that occurs in green plants, during which the green pigment chlorophyll uses light **energy** to make **carbohydrates**.

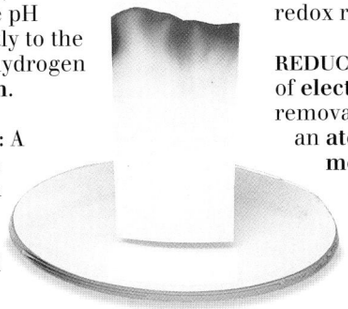

PAPER CHROMATOGRAPHY

POLYMER: A large **molecule** that is formed by the joining of smaller molecules – units called monomers – in a reaction called polymerization.

PRECIPITATE: A solid substance formed by a **chemical reaction** taking place in a **solution**. Precipitates often form during **double decomposition** reactions.

PRODUCT: An **element** or **compound** that is formed in a **chemical reaction**.

PROTEIN: An **organic polymer** that contains carbon, hydrogen, oxygen, and nitrogen. Most proteins also contain sulfur.

PROTON: A particle with a positive **electric charge**, which is found in the **nucleus** of every **atom**. The charge on a proton is exactly the opposite of that on an **electron**.

RADICAL: An **ion**, normally consisting of two or more non-metals, that generally remains unchanged during a **chemical reaction**. An example is the carbonate ion, CO_3^{2-}.

RAM: Abbreviation for relative atomic mass. It is the mass of an **atom** of an **element** relative to $^1/_{12}$ of the atomic mass of the carbon **isotope**, carbon-12. RAMs are average values, weighted for the relative natural abundances of different isotopes of an element.

RATE OF REACTION: How quickly a **chemical reaction** proceeds. It depends upon various factors, including **temperature**, and may be increased by using a **catalyst**.

REACTANT: An **element** or **compound** that is the starting material of a **chemical reaction**.

REACTIVITY: A measure of the ease with which an **atom**, an **ion**, or a **molecule** reacts. **Elements** in groups 1 and 17 of the periodic table are generally the most reactive.

REDOX REACTION: Any **chemical reaction** involving the transfer of **electrons** (**reduction** and **oxidation**). Nearly all reactions can be seen as redox reactions.

REDUCTION: The addition of **electrons** to, or the removal of oxygen from an **atom**, an **ion**, or a **molecule**. The **oxidation number** of an **element** that is reduced decreases.

REVERSIBLE REACTION: A **chemical reaction** in which the **products** can react to form the **reactants** once again. Many reactions that seem to proceed in only one direction are reversible reactions with an **equilibrium** position very close to the products.

RMM: Abbreviation for relative molecular mass. It is the sum of the **RAMs** of the **elements** that make up a **compound**. The RMM of water, H_2O, is 18, because the RAMs of hydrogen and oxygen are 1 and 16 respectively.

SALT: An **ionic compound** that is formed whenever an **acid** and a **base** react together.

SEMIMETAL: Also called a metalloid, an **element** that shows characteristics between those of metals and nonmetals. Semimetals are fairly good conductors of heat and electricity.

SOLUTE: Dissolves in a **solvent** to form a **solution**.

SOLUTION: An even **mixture** of two or more substances in which the particles involved are **atoms**, **ions**, or **molecules**. The **solvent** – a solid, liquid, or gas – dissolves one or more other substances (the **solutes**) to form a solution.

SOLVENT: Dissolves a **solute** to form a **solution**.

SPECTROMETER: Every **element** or **compound** produces a unique spectrum, or identifying pattern corresponding to **energy** levels in its **atoms**, **ions**, or **molecules**. A spectrometer is an instrument used to produce a spectrum for chemical analysis. Spectroscopes are spectrometers that use light. A mass spectrometer operates on a different principle – it is used to identify compounds by establishing their **RMMs**.

STP: Abbreviation for standard temperature and pressure. STP equals 0°C (32°F) and atmospheric pressure (101,325 Nm^{-2}).

SUSPENSION: A type of **mixture** in which particles, larger than those in a **colloid**, are unevenly distriuted in a liquid or a gas. Suspensions can be separated by **filtration**. Muddy water contains soil particles in suspension.

TEMPERATURE: A measure of how hot or cold a substance is. The temperature of a substance is directly related to the average **kinetic energy** of its **atoms**, **ions**, or **molecules**.

TITRATION: A procedure in which a measured amount of one solution of known **concentration** is added to another solution, usually in order to determine the latter's concentration.

TRANSITION METAL: Those **elements** that are found in the d- and f-blocks of the periodic table. Most metals, including iron and copper, are transition metals.

WATER OF CRYSTALLIZATION: Water that is held in **crystals** of a **compound**.

PRECIPITATION REACTION

Index

A

Acetylsalicylic acid 56
Acid salts 24, 25
Acids 22–3
  and alkali metals 36
  ammonia fountain 31
  definition 57
  fatty acids 37
  neutralization 23
  pH scale 22
  reaction rates 18, 19
  reactive metals 32, 33
  salts 24
  voltaic cells 35
Acrylic
  structure 56
Actinides 40
  periodic table 12–13
Actinium 12
Activation energy 28, 57
Activity series 32–3
Adenine 53
Aerosols
  CFCs 49
Air
  diatomic molecules 15
  gases 44
  mixture 8
  nitrogen 44
  noble gases 44
  oxygen 46
Alcohol
  fermentation 26, 27
  formula 56
  paper chromatography 8
Alkali metals 36–7
  periodic table 12–13
Alkaline dry cells 34
Alkaline earth metals 38–9
  periodic table 12–13
Alkalis 22
  ammonia fountain 31
  ammonia production 44
  definition 57
  neutralization of acids 23
  preparation of acid salts 25
  pH scale 22
  solutions 36
Alkanes
  combustion 21
  definition 57
  fractional distillation 51
  hydrocarbons 50
Alkenes 50, 57
Alkynes 50, 57
Allotropes
  carbon 42
  definition 57
  phosphorus 44
  sulfur 46, 47
Alloys
  definition 57
  iron 40
  tin 42, 43
Alpha (α) sulfur 47
Aluminum
  in Earth's crust 56
  element 6
  formula 56
  periodic table 13
  powder 14
  reactivity 32
  thermite reaction 28, 29
Aluminum oxide
  6, 14, 29, 32
Americium 13
Ammonia
  dissolution in water 30
  fountain experiment 2, 31
  Haber process 44, 45
  ions 44
  laboratory production 44, 45
  molecules 6
  nitrogen compound 44
  pH scale 22
Ammonium 56
Ammonium chloride 34, 45
Ammonium hydroxide 54, 55
Ammonium ion 44
Ammonium nitrate 28
Amylases 27
Analysis 8, 54–5
Angles
  bond 6
  sp^3 orbital 43
Anhydrous compounds 30, 57
Anhydrous copper sulfate
  21, 30
Anions
  chemical reactions 18
  definition 57
  halogens 48
  nonmetals 14
  salts 24
  testing for 55
Anodes
  definition 57
  Downs Process 15
  electrodes 35
  electrolytic cells 34
  electroplating 35
Antimony 13
Anti-suck-back device 23, 48
Aqueous solutions 2
  acids and bases 22
  chemical analysis 54
  definition 57
  nickel nitrate 8
  sucrose 52
Argon
  in air 8, 44
  periodic table 13
Arsenic 13
Artificial elements
  periodic table 13
Ascorbic acid 56
Ash
  magnesium oxide 15
Aspirin 56
Astatine 13, 48
Atmosphere
  ozone layer 48, 49
Atomic force microscopes
  16, 57
Atomic number 10
  definition 57
  periodic table 12
Atoms 10–11
  activity series 32–3
  alkali metals 36
  alkaline earth metals 38
  atomic diameter 36
  Avogadro's constant 11
  bonds 16–17
  boron 10
  buckminsterfullerene 42
  carbon 42, 52
  chemical reactions 18
  compounds 6
  definition 57
  displacement reactions 32–3
  electrochemistry 34
  electron shells 10
  electrons 10
  elements 6
  gas molar volume 11
  graphite 42
  halogens 48
  heat 28
  metals 14
  mole 10
  molecular orbitals 16, 17
  neutrons 10
  nonmetals 14
  nucleus 10
  orbitals 10
  organic chemistry 50, 52
  oxidation 20, 21
  oxidation number 20
  protons 10
  reduction 20
  relative atomic mass
  (RAM) 10
  relative molecular mass
  (RMM) 10
  water 30
Avogadro's constant 11

B

Bacteria
  chlorination of water 48
Baking powder 36
Balard, Antoine-Jérôme 56
Ball and stick models 6
Barium
  barium meals 38, 39
  flame tests 2, 54
  periodic table 12, 38
Barium carbonate 43
Barium sulfate 39
Bases 22
  alkalis 22
  definition 57
  salts 24
  sodium hydroxide 36
Bases
  genetic code 52, 53
Basic oxygen process
  manufacture of steel 40, 41
Batteries 34, 35
Berkelium 13
Beryllium 12, 38
Biochemistry 53
Bismuth 13
Blast furnaces 41
Bleach 48, 49
  formula 56
Blood
  hemoglobin 53
  red blood cells 52
Blue pigments
  paper chromatography 8
Boiling points 56
Bonds
  angles 6
  atoms 16–17
  carbon atoms 52
  covalent 16–17
  hydrocarbons 50
  hydrogen bonding 16, 17
  ionic 16
  molecular models 6
  organic chemistry 50
  surface catalysis 26
Boron
  atoms 10
  periodic table 13
Brandt, Georg 56
Brass
  electroplating 35
Bread
  rising agents 37
Breathalyzers 8
Brine 36, 37
Bromide 56
Bromine 48
  boiling point 56
  discovery of 56
  mass spectrometry 55
  melting point 56
  periodic table 13, 48
  photocatalysis 26
Bronze 42, 43
Buckminsterfullerene 6, 42
Bunsen burners
  flame tests 54
Burning
  activation energy 28
  chemical reaction 21
  definition 57
  hydrocarbons 50
  magnesium 15
  oxidation 20
  oxygen 46
But-1-ene 50
But-1-yne 50
But-2-ene 50
But-2-yne 50
Butane 50
  fractional distillation 51
Butene
  isomers 50
Butyne
  isomers 50

C

Cadmium 13
Calcium
  compounds 38
  in Earth's crust 56
  flame tests 54
  formula 56
  glass 43
  hard water 38
  ions 38
  mortar 39
  periodic table 12, 38
  reactivity 32
Calcium carbide 50
Calcium carbonate
  formula 56
  glass 43
  hard water 38
  limestone 25
  manufacture of steel 41
  marble 19
  mortar 39
Calcium chloride 15, 28
Calcium
  hydrogencarbonate 38
Calcium hydroxide
  ammonia production
  44, 45
  mortar 39
  preparation of ethyne 50
  testing for carbon
  dioxide 21
  testing for carbonates 54
Calcium oxide 45
Calcium sulfate
  hemihydrate 56
Californium 13
Candle wax
  combustion 21
  fractional distillation 51
  melting point 16
Carbohydrates 52, 57
Carbon 42
  allotropes 42
  alloys 40, 57
  atoms 52
  boiling point 56
  catalytic cracking of oil 51
  combustion 21
  compounds 6
  dehydration of sucrose 30
  discovery of 56
  DNA 53
  ethanol 6
  extraction of iron 15
  fatty acids 37
  fractional distillation 51
  fullerenes 42
  hydrocarbons 50
  melting point 56
  molecular structure of
  diamond 5, 42
  organic chemistry 42, 50, 52
  periodic table 13, 42
Carbon dioxide
  acid on a
  hydrogencarbonate 23
  acid on limestone 25
  carbonated drinks 27
  catalytic converters 27
  chemical reactions 19
  and combustion 21
  dry ice 28
  extraction of iron 15
  fermentation 27
  and mortar 39
  photosynthesis 38
  sodium
  hydrogencarbonate 37
  testing for carbonates 54
Carbon monoxide 27
Carbonated drinks 27
Carbonates 23
  formula 56
  rocks 25
  salts 24
  testing for 54
Cars
  catalytic converters 26, 27
Catalysts 26–7
  catalytic cracking of oil 51
  CFCs 49
  copper oxide 40
  decomposition of
  hydrogen peroxide 46
  definition 57
  Haber process 45
  hydrocarbons 50
Catalytic converters 26, 27
Cathodes
  definition 57
  Downs Process 15
  electrolytic cells 34
  electroplating 35
Cathodic protection 33
Cations
  acid salts 25
  activity series 32
  alkali metals 36
  alkaline earth metals 38
  ammonium ion 44
  chemical reactions 18
  definition 57
  electrodes 35
  flame tests 54
  metals 14
  salts 24
  testing for 55
Cavendish, Henry 56
Cells
  electrochemical 34–5
  red blood cells 52
Cement 8, 38
Cerium 12
Cesium 12, 36
CFCs (chlorofluorocarbons)
  48, 49
  definition 57
Chalk 56
Charcoal 42
Charge *see* Electric charge
Charged particles 34
Chemical analysis 8, 54–5
Chemical balances 11
Chemical reactions 18–19
  acid-base 22
  atoms 6
  catalysts 26–7
  combustion 21, 46
  conservation of mass 19
  decomposition 7, 18
  definition 57
  displacement 5, 32–3
  electrochemistry 34
  endothermic 28, 58
  energy changes 28
  exothermic 14, 15, 21, 28
  extraction of metals 15
  iron sulfide 7
  molecular model 5
  oxidation 20–1
  reaction rates 18, 19
  redox 15, 20–1
  reduction 20–1
  reversible 5, 41, 45
  thermite 29
  titration 23
Chemical symbols 13
Chips
  silicon 42
Chloride
  chemical reactions 19
  formation of sodium
  chloride 17
  formula 56
  salts 24
Chlorine
  bleaching 49
  CFCs 49
  characteristics 14
  chloroethene 53
  compounds 48
  concentrations 48
  discovery of 56
  Downs Process 15
  gas 28, 48
  halogen 48
  macromolecules 14
  mass spectrometry 55
  periodic table 13, 48
  preparation 48
  sodium hydroxide 37
  in water 48, 49
Chlorine monoxide 49
Chloroethene 53, 56
Chlorofluorocarbons

see CFCs
Chlorophyll 2, 38
Chromate ion 41
Chromatography 54
definition 57
gas chromatography 8
paper chromatography 4, 8
separating mixtures 8
Chromium
alloys 40
discovery of 56
oxidation number 40, 41
periodic table 12
Chromium oxides 40
Cobalt
chemical reactions 19
discovery of 56
periodic table 12
Cobalt chloride 5, 11
Colloids 8, 57
Color
alkaline earth metals 39
bleaching 49
chemical analysis 55
chlorine test kit 49
fireworks 39
flame tests 54
glass 43
metals 14
paper chromatography 4, 8
transition metals 40
Combustion reaction 21
hydrocarbons 50
oxygen 46
Comparitors 49
Complex ions 19
chlorine in water 49
definition 57
Compounds 6–7, 8
anhydrous 30
bonds 16
calcium 38
chemical analysis 54
chlorine 48
copper 40
decomposition 7
definition 57
dehydrating agents 30
efflorescent 30, 31
exothermic reactions 28
hygroscopic 30, 31
ionic 2, 5
macromolecules 14
metals 14
nitrogen 44
organic chemistry 50
oxidation number 20
relative molecular mass (RMM) 10
salts 24
sodium 36
sp hybrid orbitals 42
sulfur 46
transition metals 40
water and 30
Concentrations 10
chemical reactions 18, 19
chlorine 48
definition 57
solutions 11
titration 23
Condensation
fractional distillation 51
Condenser jacket 9
Conductors
electrochemistry 34
metal 14
Conservation of mass 19
Copper 14
bronze 43
compounds 40
displacement reactions 32–3
electrodes 35
electroplating 35
formula 56
molar mass 11
oxidation 20
periodic table 13
preparation of nitrogen 44
reactivity 32
transition metals 40
Copper carbonate 40
Copper chloride 2, 40
Copper hydroxide 40
Copper nitrate 33, 40
Copper oxide 24, 40
Copper sulfate
anhydrous 21
displacement reactions 32
formation 24
solution 2
water of crystallization 30
Corrosion 32, 33
Covalent bonds 5, 16–17
definition 57
ethyne 50
Cracking
hydrocarbons 50, 51
Crude oil 50, 51
Crystals
definition 57
hydrated 5
ionic compounds 2
macromolecules 17
potassium permanganate 1
rhombic sulfur 47
silicon 42
sucrose 52
water of crystallization 30, 31
Curium 13
Current, electric 34, 35
Cytosine 53

D

D-block
periodic table 40
D-orbitals 10
Decomposition 18
catalytic cracking of oil 51
definition 57
double decomposition reaction 55
electrolytic 34
fermentation 27
flame tests 54
mercury oxide 7
preparation of oxygen 46
sodium hydrogencarbonate 37
Dehydrating agents 30, 57
Deoxyribonucleic acid (DNA) 52, 53
Deposition, reactivity 32
Desiccators 30, 31
Detergent
laundry 27
1,6-diaminohexane 2, 52
Diamond
carbon atoms 42
molecular structure 5
Diatomic molecules
definition 57
electrolytic decomposition of water 34
gases 48
nitrogen monoxide 18
oxygen 15, 18
surface catalysis 26
Digestion
starch 27
Digestive system
X-rays 38, 39
Dioxides
silicon 6
Disaccharides 52
Displacement reactions 5, 32–3
definition 57
Distillation
definition 57
fractional 51
solutions 8, 9
Distilled water 22
DNA (deoxyribonucleic acid) 52, 53
Dobson Units 49
Double bonds
organic chemistry 50
Double decomposition
definition 57
reaction 18, 55
Downs Process
sodium production 14, 15
Dreschel bottles 48
Dry cells 34
Dry ice 28
Drying agents 31, 48
Drying towers 45
Ductility
metals 14
Dysprosium 13

E

Earth
elements in crust 56
ozone layer 48, 49
Earth metals
alkaline 38–9
periodic table 12–13
Efflorescent
compounds 30, 31
definition 57
Einsteinium 13
Electric charge
atoms 34
definition 57
ionic bonding 16
mass spectrometry 54
Electric circuits 43
Electrical energy
reactions 28
Electrical forces
atomic 10
Electricity
conductors 14
Electrochemical cell 34, 58
Electrochemistry 34–5
Electrodes 34, 35, 58
Electrolysis 34
definition 58
Downs Process 15
sodium hydroxide 36, 37
Electrolytes 34
definition 58
electroplating 35
Electrolytic cells 34
Electromotive force 34
Electron shell
alkali metals 36
covalent bonding 16
definition 58
halogens 48
periodic table 12
Electronics 42
Electrons 10
activity series 32
alkali metals 36
alkaline earth metals 38, 39
current 34
definition 58
electron shells 10
halogens 48
ionic bonding 16
isotopes 10
metals 14
orbitals 10
oxidation 20, 21
periodic table 12
reduction 20
Electroplating 35, 58
Electrostatic attraction 16
Elements 6–7
alkali metals 36
alkaline earth metals 38
atomic number 10
compounds 6
definition 58
discovery of 56
Earth's crust 56
flame tests 54
halogens 48
isotopes 10
melting points 56
metals 14–15
mixtures 8
nitrogen 44
nonmetals 14
organic chemistry 50
oxidation number 20
oxygen 46
periodic table 12–13
phosphorus 44
sulfur 46
transition metals 40
water and 30
Elhuyar, Fausto 56
Elhuyar, Juan José 56
Endothermic reactions 28, 58
Energy
activation energy 28
decomposition 7
definition 58
extracting metals from ores 14
fireworks 39
heat 28–9
kinetic 28, 58
melting points 16
photosynthesis 38
Enzymes
catalysts 26
definition 58
digestion of starch 27
fermentation 27
powdered laundry detergent 27
Equilibrium
chemical reactions 18, 19
definition 58
Erbium 13
Ethane 50, 51
Ethanoic acid 56
Ethanol 6, 56
Ethene 50, 56
Ethyne 50, 51
Europium 13
Exothermic reactions
burning 15, 21, 28
definition 58
formation of sodium chloride 14
preparation of ethyne 50
Explosives 44
Extraction
metals 14, 15

F

F-block
periodic table 40
Fabrics
bleaching 49
Fats
production of soap 37
Fatty acids 36, 37
Fermentation 26, 27
Fermium 13
Fertilizers 44
Films
photographic 47
Filter paper 8, 9
Filtration 8
definition 58
muddy water 9
Fire bricks 15
Fireworks 38, 39
Fixer
sodium thiosulfate 47
Flame tests 2, 54
Fluoride
formula 56
ions 48
Fluorine
CFCs 49
covalent bonding 17
ionic bonding 16
periodic table 13, 48
"Fool's gold" 6
Forces
atomic 10
Formulae 56
Fountain experiment
ammonia 31
Fractional distillation 8, 51
Fractionating towers 50, 51
Francium 12, 36
Friction
activation energy 28
Fructose 27
Fruit
sugars 27
Fullerenes 42
Furnaces
fractional distillation 51
manufacture of steel 41

G

Gadolinium 13
Galena 6
Gallium 13
Gas chromatography 8
Gas mantles 16
Gases
air 8, 44
chlorine 14, 48
as liquids 28
mixtures 8
molar volume 11
nitrogen 44
nonmetals 14
oxygen 46
periodic table 12
water and 30
Gasoline
fractional distillation 51
Genetic code
DNA 52, 53
Germanium 13, 42
Glass 42, 43
Glucose 27, 52
Glycerol
fatty acids 37
Gold
atoms 16
boiling point 56
discovery of 56
element 6
melting point 56
periodic table 13
reactivity 32
transition metals 40
Graphite 6
atoms 16, 42
Guanine 53
Gunpowder 39

H

Haber, Fritz 45
Haber process
ammonia production 44, 45
Hafnium 12
Halide ions 48, 55
Halogens 48–9
chemical analysis 55
Hard water 24, 38
Heat 28–9
conductors 14
decomposition 7
endothermic reactions 28
exothermic reactions 28
extraction of metals 15
fireworks 39
thermite reaction 29
Hemoglobin 52, 53
Helium
boiling point 56
discovery of 56
gas chromatography 8
melting point 56
periodic table 13
Hexane 2, 52
Hexanedioic acid 2, 52
Holmium 13
Hybrid orbitals 17, 42, 43
Hybridization 58
Hydrated cobalt chloride 11
Hydrated copper chloride 2
Hydrated crystals 5, 30
Hydrated iron oxide 20, 56
Hydrocarbons
bonds 50
catalytic converters 27
combustion 21
cracking 50, 51
definition 58
fractional distillation 51
organic chemistry 50
Hydrochloric acid
chemical reactions 19
pH scale 22
preparation 23
preparation of chlorine 48
preparation of hydrogen sulfide 47
Hydrogen
acid salts 24, 25
acids 22

ammonia 6, 44, 45
bonding 16, 17, 58
and combustion 21
covalent bonding 17
dehydrating agents 30
discovery of 56
DNA 53
in Earth's crust 56
electrolytic decomposition of water 34
ethanol 6
fatty acids 37
formula 56
hydrocarbons 50
periodic table 12
pH scale 22
reaction of sodium with water 36
reactivity of metals 33
salts 24
voltaic cells 35
water 6, 30
Hydrogen chloride 22, 23
Hydrogen fluoride 17
Hydrogen oxide 56
Hydrogen peroxide 46
Hydrogen sulfide 46, 47
Hydrogencarbonate
acid on 23
formula 56
testing for 54
Hydronium
formula 56
ions 22, 33, 58
Hydroxide
anions 36
bases 22
formula 56
ions 22
salts 24
Hygroscopic
compounds 30, 31
definition 58
"Hypo" 47

I

Indicator
definition 58
pH scale 22
Indium 13
Inert elements 12
Ink
paper chromatography 8
Iodide 56
Iodine 6, 48
mass spectrometry 55
molar mass 11
periodic table 13, 48
starch indicator 27
Ionic bonding 16
definition 58
lithium fluoride 16
metals 14
Ionic compounds 2, 5
Ions
acids 22
activity series 32
alkali metals 36
alkaline earth metals 38
ammonia 44
chemical analysis 54
chemical reactions 18
chlorine in water 49
complex ions 19, 57
definition 58
displacement reactions 32–3
electrochemistry 34
formula and charge 56
halogens 48
heat 28
hydronium 22
ionic diameter 36
macromolecules 14, 17
mass spectrometry 54, 55
metals 2
mole 10
oxidation 20
reduction 20
salts 24, 25
solutions 8
transition metals 40
Iridium 12
Iron
alloys 40
boiling point 56
catalyst 26, 45
chemical reactions 7
in Earth's crust 56
extraction 14, 15
formula 56
hemoglobin 53
iron and sulfur mixture 7
iron sulfide 6
manufacture of steel 41
melting point 56
ores 15
oxidation number 20
periodic table 12
pyrites 6
reactivity 6, 32
rusting 20
thermite reaction 29
transition metals 40
Iron oxide
extraction of iron 14, 15
glass 43
thermite reaction 29
Iron sulfide 7, 47
Isomers
carbon compounds 50
Isotopes
atomic number 10
definition 58

J

Janssen, Pierre 56

K

Kerosene
fractional distillation 51
Kinetic energy 28, 58
Krypton 13

L

Laboratory tests
chemical analysis 54
Lanthanides
periodic table 12–13, 40
Lanthanum 12
Lather
soap 38
Laundry detergent
powdered 27
Lawrencium 13
Lead
flame tests 2, 54
lead shot 6
periodic table 13, 42
reactivity 32
solder 43
Lead iodide 18
Lead nitrate 18
Lead oxide 19, 40
"Lead" pencils 42
Lead sulfide 6
Leaves
photosynthesis 38
Life
polymers 52
Light
as a catalyst 26
energy 28
fireworks 39
photosynthesis 38
Lime
slaked 39
Limestone
acid on 25
formula 56
manufacture of steel 41
mineral water 24
Limewater 21, 54
Liquids
distillation 8, 9
gases as 28
mixtures 8
Litharge 40
Lithium
atomic diameter 36
cation 36
ionic bonding 16
ionic diameter 36
periodic table 12, 36
Lithium fluoride 16
Litmus paper
ammonia fountain 31
reaction of sodium with water 36
Lockyer, Joseph Norman 56
Luster
metals 14
Lutetium 13

M

Macromolecules
crystals 17
definition 58
ionic bonding 14, 16
Magnesite bricks 41
Magnesium
atoms 15
burning 15
in chlorophyll 2, 38
ductility 14
in Earth's crust 56
fireworks 39
formula 56
periodic table 12, 38
reactivity 32
reactivity with dilute acids 33
thermite reaction 29
Magnesium oxide 15
Magnetic field
mass spectrometry 55
Magnets 7
Malleability
metals 14
Manganese
periodic table 12
preparation of oxygen 46
Manganese chloride 49
Manganese oxide 49
alkaline dry cells 34
preparation of chlorine 48
Marble 18, 19
Mass
Avogadro's constant 11
chemical reactions 18, 19
conservation of 19
molar mass 11
relative atomic mass (RAM) 10
relative molecular mass (RMM) 10
Mass spectrometry 54, 55
Matches
activation energy 28
Melting points 16, 56
Mendelevium 13
Mercury
boiling point 56
element 6
melting point 56
periodic table 13
reactivity 32
thermometers 9
Mercury cathode process
sodium hydroxide 37
Mercury oxide 6, 7
Metals 14–15
activity series 32–3
alkali metals 36–7
alkaline earth metals 38–9
atoms 14
catalysts 26
cations 14
characteristics 14
color 14
compounds 14
corrosion 32, 33
electrodes 35
electrons 14
electroplating 34, 35
extraction 15
flame tests 2, 54
macromolecules 14
ores 14
oxides 14
and oxygen 15
periodic table 12–13
reactive 14
salts 24
thermite reaction 28, 29
transition metals 5, 40–1
welding 28, 29
Methane 50, 51
Methanol 56
Methyl orange indicators 23
Methylated spirits 56
Microelectronics
silicon chips 42
Microscopes
atomic force 16, 57
Milk
colloid 8
Mineral water 24, 25
Mixtures 8–9
chemical analysis 54
colloids 8
decomposition 18
definition 58–9
dehydrating agents 30
distillation 9
filtration 8, 9
hydrocarbons 50
iron and sulfur 7
solutions 8
suspensions 8
Models
molecular 6
Molarity 11
Mole 10
Avogadro's constant 11
definition 59
gas molar volume 11
molar mass 11
molar solutions 11
Molecular orbitals
covalent bonds 17
definition 59
electron shells 16
Molecules 10–11
acids 22
bonding 16
carbon 52
chloroethene 53
chlorophyll 2, 38
compounds 6
definition 59
diatomic 15, 18
extraction of metals 15
gas molar volume 11
heat 28
macromolecules 14
models 6
mole 10
molecular model of reaction 5
molecular structure of diamond 5
polymerization 52
relative molecular mass (RMM) 10
surface catalysis 26
water 30
Molten sulfur 47
Molybdenum 12
Monoclinic (β) sulfur 47
Monohydrates 31
Monomers 53, 56
Monosaccharides 52
Mortar 38, 39
Muddy water, filtration 9

N

Naphtha
fractional distillation 51
Neodymium 12
Neon 13
Neptunium 12
Networks
fullerenes 42
Neutralization of acids 23
Neutrons 10
boron 10
definition 59
isotopes 10
relative atomic mass (RAM) 10
Nickel
catalysts 26
element 6
periodic table 13
Nickel nitrate 8
Niobium 12
Nitrate 56
Nitric acid 44
oxidation of copper 20
preparation of nitrogen dioxide 3
Nitrogen 44–5
in air 8
ammonia 6, 44, 45
boiling point 56
catalytic converters 27
chlorophyll 38
compounds 44
DNA 53
melting point 56
molecular model of chlorophyll 2
nitric acid 20
periodic table 13, 44
preparation 44
Nitrogen dioxide
decomposition 18
oxidation number 20
preparation 3, 20
Nitrogen monoxide 18
Nitrogen oxides 18, 20, 27
Nobelium 13
Noble gases
in air 44
definition 59
periodic table 12, 13
reactions with halogens 48
Nonmetals
atoms 14
carbon 42
characteristics 14
periodic table 12–13
salts 24
Nonane
fractional distillation 51
Nucleus 10
atomic number 12
boron 10
definition 59
electron shells 10
Nylon
formation of 2, 52
polymers 52

O

Oil (crude)
catalytic cracking 51
fractional distillation 51
hydrocarbons 50
Oils
production of soap 37
Orbitals
definition 59
electrons 10
hybrid 17, 42, 43
molecular 16, 17
periodic table 12
Ores 14
definition 59
iron 15
Organic chemistry 50-3
carbon 42
definition 59
Osmium 12
Oxidation 20–1
bleaching 49
definition 59
electrolytic cells 34
preparation of chlorine 48
transition metals 40
voltaic cells 35
Oxidation number 20, 59
Oxides
bases 22
formula 56
iron 15
metals 14
salts 24
thermite reaction 28, 29
Oxygen 46
in air 8, 44, 46
boiling point 56
combustion 15, 21, 46

dehydrating agents 30
diatomic molecules 15, 18
in Earth's crust 56
electrolytic decomposition of water 34
ethanol 6
extraction of iron 15
fatty acids 37
hemoglobin 52, 53
hydrogen bonding 17
laboratory preparation 46
melting point 56
mercury oxide 7
metal oxides 14
metals and 15
molecular model of chlorophyll 2
nitrogen dioxide 18
oxidation 20
ozone depletion reactions 49
periodic table 13, 46
reactivity 32
rusting of iron 20
test for 46
thermite reaction 29
water 6, 30
Ozone layer 48, 49

P

P-orbitals 10
covalent bonding 17
hybrid orbitals 17, 43
ionic bonding 16
Palladium 13
Paper
filter 8, 9
Paper chromatography 4, 8
Paraffin oil
fractional distillation 51
Particles
colloids 8
distillation 9
filtration 9
gas molar volume 11
heat 28
mixtures 8
solutions 8
suspensions 8
Patina
bronze 43
Pencil "lead" 42
Periodic table 12–13
alkali metals 36
alkaline earth metals 38
carbon 42
halogens 48
nitrogen 44
oxygen 46
phosphorus 44
silicon 42
sulfur 46
tin 42
transition metals 40
pH scale 22, 59
Phenylethene 56
Phosphate 53
Phosphorus 44
activation energy 28
allotropes 44
periodic table 13, 44
Photocatalysis 26
Photography
catalysts 26
sodium thiosulfate 46, 47
Photosynthesis
catalysts 26
chlorophyll 38
definition 59
Phytol 38
Picometers 36
Pigments
bleaching 49
paper chromatography 4, 8
pH scale 22
transition metals 40
Plants
chlorophyll 38
photosynthesis 26, 38, 59
Plaster of Paris 56
Plastic sulfur 47
Plastics 52, 56
Platinum
catalytic converters 27
discovery of 56
flame tests 2, 55
periodic table 13
reactivity 32
reactivity with dilute acids 33
transition metal 40
Plutonium 12
Pollution
catalytic converters 26, 27
Polonium 13
Poly(chloroethene) (PVC) 53, 56
Poly(ethene) 56
Polymerization 52, 53
Polymers 52, 59
Poly(phenylethene) 56
Poly(propenonitrile) 56
Polysaccharides 52
Polystyrene 56
Poly(tetrafluoroethene) 56
Polyethylene 52, 56
Poor metals
periodic table 12–13
Porphyrin ring
chlorophyll 38
Potassium
atomic diameter 36
in Earth's crust 56
flame tests 54
ionic diameter 36
ionic formula 56
periodic table 12, 36
reactivity 32
Potassium chromate 5, 41
Potassium dichromate 41
Potassium iodide 18
Potassium nitrate 18
Potassium permanganate 1
Potatoes
digestion of starch 27
Praseodymium 12
Precipitates
chemical analysis 54
chemical reactions 18
definition 59
Pressure
standard temperature and pressure (STP) 11
Product
chemical reactions 18, 59
Promethium 12
Propane 50, 51
Propene 50
Propenonitrile 56
Properties 6, 7
chemical reactions 18
Propyne 50
Protactinium 12
Proteins
definition 59
enzymes 26
hemoglobin 53
powdered laundry detergent 27
Protons 10
acids 22
atomic number 10, 12
bases 22
boron 10
definition 59
isotopes 10
relative atomic mass (RAM) 10
PTFE 56
Ptyalin 26, 27
PVC 52, 56
Pyrite
iron 6

Q

Quartz
crystals 6
glass 43
silicon 42, 43
Quicklime 43

R

Radiation
ozone layer 48, 49
Radicals
definition 59
flame tests 54
formula and charge 56
salts 24, 25
Radium 12, 38
Radon 13
Rainwater 24, 25
RAM *see* Relative atomic mass
Rare earth metals
periodic table 12–13
Rate of reaction 59
Reactants 18
conservation of mass 19
definition 59
surface area 19
Reactions *see* Chemical reactions
Reactivity
activity series 32–3
definition 59
halogens 48
metals 14
Red blood cells 52
Red lead 19
Red phosphorus 44
Red pigments
paper chromatography 8
Redox reactions 20–1
combustion 46
definition 59
extraction of metals 15
reactivity 32
Reduction 20–1
definition 59
electrolytic cells 34
Refineries
oil 51
Relative atomic mass (RAM) 10
copper 11
definition 59
iodine 11
periodic table 13
Relative molecular mass (RMM) 10, 59
Reversible reactions 5, 18
ammonia production 45
chromate ions 41
definition 59
Rhenium 12
Rhodium
catalytic converters 27
periodic table 12
Rhombic sulfur 46, 47
Rings
sulfur 46, 47
RMM *see* Relative molecular mass
Rocks
carbonate 25
quartz 42, 43
Rubidium
atomic diameter 36
ionic diameter 36
periodic table 12, 36
Rust 20, 56
Ruthenium 12

S

S-orbitals 10
covalent bonding 17
hybrid orbitals 17, 43
ionic bonding 16
Saccharides 52
Saliva 26, 27
Salt (common) 24, 36
formation of 14
formula 56
hydrogen chloride gas 23
ionic bonding 16
production of soap 37
Salts 24–5
acid salts 25
acids and bases 22
ammonium ion 44
definition 59
hard water 38
production of soap 37
reactivity 32
Samarium 12
Sand
glass 43
mortar 39
quartz 42
Scale
calcium salts 38
Scandium 12
Scheele, Carl Wilhelm 56
Seawater 8
Selenium 13
Semiconductors 42
Semimetals
definition 59
periodic table 12–13
Silica gel
desiccator 31
Silicon 42
crystals 42
in Earth's crust 56
periodic table 13, 42
Silicon chips 42
Silicon dioxide 6
Silicon oxide 42, 43
Silver
displacement reactions 5, 33
formula 56
periodic table 13
reactivity 32
reactivity with dilute acids 33
transition metals 40
Silver bromide 55
photographic films 26, 47
Silver halides 26, 47, 55
Silver nitrate
chemical analysis 54, 55
reactivity 33
Single bonds
organic chemistry 50
Slaked lime 39
Soap
hard water 38
lather 38
pH scale 22
production of 36, 37
Soda bread 37
Sodium
atomic diameter 36
boiling point 56
characteristics 14
compounds 36
Downs Process 14, 15
in Earth's crust 56
flame tests 2
formation of sodium chloride 17
formula 56
glass 43
ionic diameter 36
macromolecules 14
melting point 56
periodic table 12, 36
reaction with water 36
reactivity 32
salts 24
sodium hydroxide 37
Sodium bicarbonate 23
decomposition 37
formula 56
Sodium carbonate 43
Sodium carbonate decahydrate 31, 56
Sodium chloride 24, 36
characteristics 14
Downs Process 15
formation of 14
formula 56
ionic bonding 16
macromolecules 17
Sodium dichromate 9
Sodium hydrogencarbonate 36
decomposition 37
formula 56
reaction with acid 23
Sodium hydrogensulfate 25
Sodium hydroxide
manufacture 36, 37
neutralization of acid 23, 25
preparation of nitrogen 44
production of soap 37
Sodium hypochlorite
bleaching 48, 49
formula 56
Sodium octadecanoate 37
Sodium sulfite 47
Sodium thiosulfate 46, 47
Soil
filtering muddy water 9
Solder 42, 43
Soldering iron 43
Solids 8
Solutes
definition 59
distillation 8, 9
mixtures 8
Solutions
acids and bases 22
alkaline 36
aqueous 2, 57
calcium salts 38
chemical analysis 54
chemical reactions 18
concentration 11
definition 59
distillation 8, 9
electric charge carriers 34
filtration 9
mixtures 8
molar 11
pH scale 22
potassium permanganate 1
reactivity 32
sucrose 52
titration 23
Solvents
definition 59
distillation 8, 9
mixtures 8
water 31
Soot 21, 50
South Pole
ozone layer 49
SP hybrid orbitals 42, 43
Space-filling models 6
Spectrometry 54, 55, 59
Stainless steel 40
Standard temperature and pressure (STP) 11, 59
Starch
digestion of 27
molecules 52
Steel
alloys 40
cathodic protection 33
manufacture 41
STP *see* Standard temperature and pressure
Strontium
fireworks 39
flame tests 2
periodic table 12, 38
Structure
molecular 5
Sublimation 48
Sucrose 52
dehydration 30
formula 56
Sugars
digestion of starch 27
DNA 53
fermentation 26, 27
formula 56
molecules 52
photosynthesis 38
sucrose 52
surface catalysis 27
Sulfate
formula 56
salts 24
Sulfides 46, 56
Sulfur 46–7
allotropes 46, 47
chemical reactions 7
compounds 46
discovery of 56
iron and sulfur mixture 7
iron sulfide 6
periodic table 13, 46
rings 46, 47
sodium thiosulfate 47
Sulfuric acid
dehydrating agent 30

SHERWOOD BRANCH LIBRARY
J540 C
Challoner, Jack
The visual dictionary of
chemistry.

Defiance Public Library System
[redacted]